with compliments

Middleton Press

Middleton Press Ltd
126a Camelsdale Road
Haslemere
Surrey
GU27 3RJ

Ray Esher   Tel: 01730 813169
email: info@middletonpress.co.uk   www.middletonpress.co.uk

LANCASTER TO OXENHOLME

including the former LNWR branches
to Morecambe and Windermere

Roy Davies

MP Middleton Press

Front cover: An unidentified Virgin Trains Pendolino crossing Carlisle Bridge, Lancaster, on 12th September 2015 with a Glasgow - London Euston service. (Duncan Robert)

Back cover, upper: On 2nd July 1966 Stanier class 5 4-6-0s and Ivatt 2-6-0s stand outside Carnforth MPD. All these locomotives were allocated to the shed. Also in the photograph is an English Electric Type 4 mainline diesel locomotive and two 350hp shunters. (Ron Herbert)

Back cover, lower: Railway Clearing House map (edited), dated 1947. The route of the album is shown with a dotted line.

In memory of
Anton Cary

Published April 2023

ISBN 978 1 910356 77 7

© Middleton Press Ltd, 2023

Cover design and Photo enhancement Deborah Esher
Production & design Cassandra Morgan

Published by
    Middleton Press Ltd
    Camelsdale Road
    Haslemere
    Surrey
    GU27 3RJ
Tel: 01730 813169
Email: info@middletonpress.co.uk
www.middletonpress.co.uk

Printed and bound by CPI Group (UK) Ltd,
Croydon, CR0 4YY

Abbreviations:
British Rail (BR)
Caledonian Railway (CR)
Electro-Motive Diesel (EMD)
Furness & Midland Joint Railway (F&MJR)
Grand Junction Railway (GJR)
Great British Railways (GBR)
Kendal & Windermere Railway (K&WR)
Lancaster & Carlisle Railway (L&CR)
Lancaster & Preston Junction Railway (L&PJR)
London & Birmingham (L&BR)
London Midland and Scottish Railway (LMS)
London and North Western Railway (LNWR)
Manchester & Birmingham Railways (M&BR)
Midland Railway (MR)
North Union Railway (NUR)
North Western Railway (NWR)
Overhead Line Equipment (OLE)
West Coast Main Line (WCML)
West Coast Railways (WCR)

CONTENTS

ACKNOWLEDGEMENTS

We are very grateful for the assistance received from many of those mentioned in the credits, also from G. Croughton, R. Daniels, J. Dove, G. Gartside, T. Heavyside, S. Henson, C.M. Howard, N. Langridge, D. Richardson, D. and Dr S. Salter, P.D. Shannon, J. Shuttleworth, M. Stewart and G. Wilson.

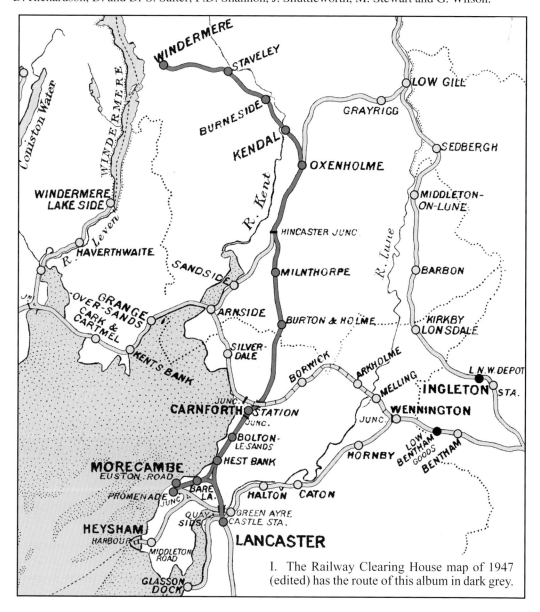

I. The Railway Clearing House map of 1947 (edited) has the route of this album in dark grey.

GEOGRAPHICAL SETTING

The line from Lancaster to Oxenholme runs more or less due north through Lancaster and on to Cumbria, formerly Westmorland, just south of Burton & Holme station and, for a large part, follows the route of the Lancaster canal. After crossing the River Lune the line drops down to the alluvial plain where the Morecambe branch diverges towards the resort on a line that is relatively flat. To the east, the land starts to rise as the coastal plain gives way to the Bowland Fells beyond the M6 motorway. The main line remains relatively flat and close to Morecambe Bay until it reaches Carnforth where it then commences the long climb up to Oxenholme through the uplands of the Southern Lakeland, part of the Lake District National Park. A feature of the limestone and sandstone uplands is rough grazing of sheep and, in the valleys, dairy cattle as well as oats and fodder crops are raised. At Oxenholme the Windermere branch diverges to the northwest; the line descends quite steeply into Kendal and starts to rise where, today, it follows the route of the A591 until it reaches its highest point between Staveley and Windermere. It then descends into the terminus that is located high above the lake.

HISTORICAL BACKGROUND

The line from Lancaster to Oxenholme forms part of the West Coast Main Line (WCML) from London to Glasgow. The section from Lancaster to Carlisle was constructed by the Lancaster & Carlisle Railway (L&CR) in association with the Caledonian Railway (CR), formed in 1847, which constructed the Carlisle to Glasgow section of the line that connected with its extensive network in Scotland. The 20 mile (32km) section of the line to Oxenholme covered by this album opened on 21st September 1846 and from there to Carlisle on 17th December 1847. The L&CR project was the largest single railway undertaking of the time and, at its peak, some 10,000 men were involved in its construction. The line was completed in two and a half years, which was remarkable given that it included the Lune crossing and significant engineering features north of Oxenholme.

Before plans for any direct rail link to Scotland had been conceived, the London & Birmingham Railway (L&BR) and the Grand Junction Railway (GJR) cornered the market in terms of rail travel to Scotland on the western side of Great Britain, albeit that half the journey was by steamer. Initially, trains ran from London to Liverpool then by steamer service to Ardrossan and, finally, a stagecoach ride to Glasgow. In 1841 the service was 'upgraded' with the opening of the North Union Railway (NUR) to Preston giving access to the port of Fleetwood, reached via the Preston & Wyre Railway.

In the mid-1830s the appetite for a railway north to Scotland was increasing and various surveys were carried out. Most notable were those by George Stephenson, the famous civil and mechanical engineer, who, in 1839, proposed two routes to Carlisle: [1] crossing Morecambe Bay on a dyke and following the Cumberland coast and [2] one that followed the Lune Valley via Shap. The coastal route was void of steep gradients but was much longer. However it had the advantage of passing a number of towns en route; plus Stephenson was reportedly wary of the capabilities of early steam locomotives. Having made some assessments of his own, civil engineer, Joseph Locke, was appointed by the GJR on 4th November 1836 to further assess a suitable route from Preston to Glasgow. He too chose a route following the Lune valley to Shap and on to Penrith and Carlisle, which included steep gradients. Understandably, the inhabitants of Kendal were not best pleased with either scheme as they both bypassed the town.

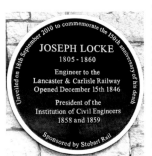

The plaque on platform 3 of Lancaster station celebrates the life and achievements of engineer, Joseph Locke. (Roy Davies)

Such was the resolve to reach Scotland by rail that the Government set up a commission (Smith & Barlow) in 1839 to determine what route the link should take. It was concerned that only one such scheme could be economical. Several routes from Lancaster to Carlisle were considered; the coastal line was rejected perhaps due to pressure from the Admiralty and, instead, the idea of a route from Lancaster to Carlisle via Kendal was favoured. With this in mind, civil engineer, George Larmer, Locke's stand-in while he was working in other areas, surveyed a route that is more or less what we know today as the WCML.

While supporting the possibility of a route north from Lancaster, the Smith & Barlow Commission still stuck to its brief that only one Anglo-Scottish route was viable but held back on giving definitive preference to either the west or east coast paths. Ultimately the Commission's opinions were becoming less relevant as the east and west coast railways were moving inexorably towards Newcastle and beyond Lancaster as plans to head towards Scotland were being realised.

On 6th November 1843 a meeting was held in Kendal and a decision was taken to build the Lancaster to Carlisle railway. The Lancaster and Carlisle Railway Company (L&CR) was set up with an authorised capital of £900,000, with subscriptions from the L&BR (£100,000), the GJR (£250,000), the NUR (£65,000) and the L&PJR (£65,000) with the balance accumulated either by way of further subscriptions or in exchange for land along the route. Joseph Locke was appointed as the Railway's eng-

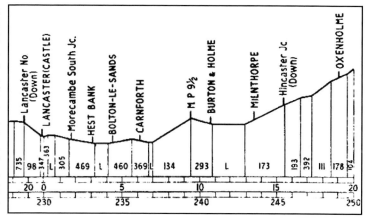

ineer. The proposed line was to leave the Penny Street terminus of the L&PJR and run east along the canal bank, crossing the Lune at Ladies Walk, heading towards Skerton Mill and on to Carnforth and the north. This proposal received Royal Assent on 6th June 1844.

What was proposed in the 1844 Bill and what transpired during construction involved two significant modifications to the plan. First, the directors of the L&CR proposed doubling the track throughout due to the likely increase in traffic, although the Caledonian Railway (CR) had not yet been incorporated, and, second, citizens of Lancaster petitioned the railway so it would run to the west of the city, thereby crossing the more commercial part of the River Lune; an amendment to the 1844 Bill received Royal Assent on 30th June 1845. The revised plans saw the line diverge from the L&PJR, at what was known as Lancaster Old Junction, just south of the Greaves Road bridge then passing through a new station, Lancaster Castle, before crossing the Lune. As plans were revealed for the line to head north, once again people in Kendal were not best pleased when they discovered that the line would pass a mile (1.6km) to the east of the town, through the village of Oxenholme. The line was planned originally to run through Kendal; hence the opening of the station in September 1846, but it would have necessitated a 2.1 mile (3km) tunnel to be built north of the town, which was deemed too expensive. However, the residents of Kendal did not come away empty-handed as plans were drawn up for construction of the Kendal & Windermere Railway (K&WR), which was adopted in the same bill as that covering the aforementioned Lancaster deviation.

Since its opening in 1846, the line between Lancaster and Oxenholme boasted five intermediate stations, namely: Hest Bank; Bolton-le-Sands; Carnforth; Burton & Holme and Milnthorpe, along with loco depots at Carnforth and Oxenholme, with the former developing into a major railway centre. All intermediate stations were closed by 1st May 1970, although Carnforth retains its Furness line platforms.

Before the line to Carlisle was completed, the L&BR, GJR and the Manchester & Birmingham Railways (M&BR) amalgamated on 16th July 1846 to form the London and North Western Railway (LNWR). In a previous agreement with the L&CR, the GJR was to operate the line on its behalf; an obligation that the newly formed LNWR assumed.

To take advantage of the burgeoning WCML, uninterrupted services were essential, which made the settlement of differences between the L&CR and the L&PJR crucial, although seemingly impossible to achieve at the time; so much so that the L&CR even contemplated constructing its own route to Preston. With the L&PJR effectively rudderless, i.e. with no constituted board of directors to negotiate with, the L&CR gave notice that it intended to run over L&PJR metals with effect from 22nd September 1846, albeit without authority. It was not a satisfactory arrangement but at least through services could run from Preston to Carlisle. As a first step to resolve the impasse, the L&CR made a record of reasonable toll charges for using the line in anticipation of matters being settled in due course.

The CR, along with the LNWR, commenced Anglo-Scottish services on 15th February 1848 linking Glasgow and Edinburgh with the northwest of England and on to Birmingham and London. Almost immediately the L&CR's revenues increased by 50% but the nagging issue of dealing with the L&PJR remained. In fact, things came to a head following a fatal accident at L&PJR's Bay Horse station on 21st August 1848; the outcome of which compelled the shareholders of the L&PJR to appoint a board of directors and enter into negotiations with the L&CR. This resulted in the latter taking over management of the L&PJR. Full amalgamation of the two companies and leasing of the K&WR were authorised by the Act of 13th August 1859.

Thanks to the Anglo-Scottish traffic the L&CR was flourishing financially and operated for some 15 years as an independent company and was able to delay absorption by the LNWR. Fearful that the L&CR's loyalty could pass to the Midland Railway, which also had plans to advance to Carlisle, the LNWR leased the L&CR for 900 years on very generous terms to its shareholders on 10th September 1859. The leasing arrangement effectively saw the end of the L&CR and the LNWR took outright ownership of it on 21st July 1879.

Under the Railways Act 1921 most of the railway companies in the UK were grouped into four main companies with effect from 1st January 1923; the London Midland and Scottish Railway (LMS) that included among many others the LNWR and CR. Following the Transport Act of 1947, the railways were nationalised and the WCML came under the control of the London Midland and Scottish Regions, which continued until privatisation of the railways (1994-97).

The Preston to Carlisle section of the WCML was electrified on 25th March 1974, utilising the 25kV overhead system, and a 'live' service through to Glasgow commenced on 6th May 1974. It is perhaps somewhat uncanny that the 25kV system used on the WCML and as a standard across Great Britain was developed on the nearby former Midland route to Morecambe. This became known as the 'Pioneer Line' after it was re-energised in 1953, but the current lines to Morecambe and Windermere have not been electrified.

In January 2000 the *Westmorland Gazette* reported that a grouping of South Lakeland businesses and local authorities known as the Northwest Partnership published a document, 'The North West Regional Strategy', that called for an investment of £20m to increase levels of railway passenger and freight transport. It was proposed that the investment would cover: reopening stations at Milnthorpe, Hest Bank and Garstang (south of Lancaster); reinstating WCML platforms at Carnforth; providing passing loops or partially reinstating a stretch of double track at Oxenholme, allowing more trains to run to Windermere, and developing regular express links between Lancaster, Barrow and Windermere. Indications were that the £20m fell far short of what would be required to fund these improvements, which is probably why none of these have occurred.

The likelihood that the WCML north from Wigan will see HS2 services in the medium term continues to diminish. First there was the scrapping of the Golborne Spur, which was to be part of HS2 that would diverge from the main line before Manchester Airport and connecting to the WCML south of Wigan. In March 2023 the Government announced that construction of the line between Birmingham and Crewe would be delayed by two years in order to cut costs. Indications are that Lancaster and Oxenholme are now unlikely to benefit from high-speed services until the 2040s at the earliest.

Morecambe Branch

In 1846 the Morecambe Harbour and Railway Company, a constituent of the North Western Railway (NWR) proposed the construction of a branch to the L&CR at Hest Bank but the idea was abandoned due to the high cost involved. In 1858 the L&CR reconsidered the idea and use of an improved Morecambe Harbour in order to export minerals from the northeast of the country carried by the South Durham & Lancashire Union Railway and the L&CR main line. The scheme met opposition from the NWR because it would lose its monopoly in serving the town but its precarious financial condition led it to concede to the L&CR's plan on condition that the called for improvements to the harbour be waived. In August 1864 the 3 mile (4.8km) branch was opened and the link to Morecambe station at Northumberland Street was established. The decision not to improve Morecambe harbour was providential given its propensity to silt up and be abandoned with the opening of the deepwater harbour at Heysham that opened in 1904; moreover the mineral traffic never materialised. Congestion at Morecambe station led the LNWR, that by then had acquired the L&CR, to open its own station at Poulton Lane in November 1870, which was later closed and replaced in 1886 by the more substantial terminus at Euston Road. Such was the level of holiday and excursion traffic to the resort in 1888 that the LNWR constructed a curve to the east of Bare Lane station joining the WCML at Morecambe South Junction; this permitted direct access to Lancaster Castle and saw services further afield to Manchester, Liverpool and London. Morecambe remained a popular holiday destination, but, in the late 1950s, competition from road traffic took its toll and BR concentrated services at the former Midland terminus at Morecambe Promenade station. This precipitated the decline and eventual closure of Euston Road station. With closure of the former Midland route to passenger and freight traffic in 1967 all services ran on the former LNWR branch and all services to Heysham harbour and the Nuclear Power Station had to reverse at Morecambe Promenade. 1994 saw a further rationalisation with closure of Promenade station in February and the opening of the current Morecambe station in May, which is situated more or less at the same location as the original station at the end of Northumberland Street. With the exception of nuclear flask trains, and other ad hoc services, all traffic for Morecambe reverses at Lancaster and services for Heysham are still required to reverse at Morecambe.

Windermere Branch

Under the same Bill that saw the line from Lancaster to Oxenholme authorised, and with the station at Kendal already open, the K&WR came into being and the 10 mile (16km) branch opened in April 1847 under the supervision of engineer Joseph Locke. In the beginning there was opposition to the line from those who saw it as destruction of the Lake District landscape. One notable opponent was William Wordsworth, who wrote the sonnet below.

The line actually terminated in the settlement of Birthwaite some distance from the Lake and Bowness-on-Windermere. The K&WR was not commercially successful and the line was acquired by the LNWR in 1859. The line was built as double track throughout and boasted through services to destinations such as Morecambe (Euston Road), Manchester Exchange and London Euston. The line was reduced to single track throughout in 1973 coinciding with the electrification and re-signalling of the WCML and all freight traffic ceased in 1972. With no passing loops, the line is accessed by a train staff kept at Oxenholme station under the control of the Carlisle box. The line can only be operated by DMUs or top and tailed loco hauled services.

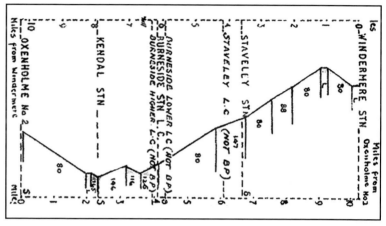

Is then no nook of English ground secure
From rash assault? Schemes of retirement sown
In youth, and 'mid the busy world kept pure
As when their earliest flowers of hope were blown,
Must perish;—how can they this blight endure?
And must he too the ruthless change bemoan
Who scorns a false utilitarian lure

'Mid his paternal fields at random thrown?
Baffle the threat, bright Scene, from Orresthead
Given to the pausing traveller's rapturous glance:
Plead for thy peace, thou beautiful romance
Of nature; and, if human hearts be dead,
Speak, passing winds; ye torrents, with your strong
And constant voice, protest against the wrong.

William Wordsworth

PASSENGER SERVICES

The majority of services were Anglo-Scottish trains running between London and Glasgow and Edinburgh, the majority of which would have stopped at Lancaster and Oxenholme as is the case today. Services to intermediate stations were sparse due mainly to lack of paths between express and freight services. 1970 saw the withdrawal of local passenger services between Lancaster and Carlisle with the consequent closure of the remaining intermediate stations, excepting Oxenholme.

Morecambe Branch

Compared with services to Promenade station, Euston Road was quieter during the winter months, but, by the late 1950s, there were regular services to/from Birmingham, Manchester and Glasgow, as well as local services to Lancaster and Preston. Today Morecambe is served by services from Leeds, including a daily boat train to Heysham port, and a shuttle from Lancaster.

Windermere Branch

In the summer months of the 1950s, there were afternoon excursions from Morecambe and Bare Lane and some Furness Line stations to Windermere for steamer services on the Lake from Bowness Pier. Until the early 1970s the branch boasted a through service from London. When withdrawn, passengers were required to take a shuttle from Oxenholme. Since privatisation the shuttle service is supplemented by through trains to Lancaster, Preston and Manchester Airport.

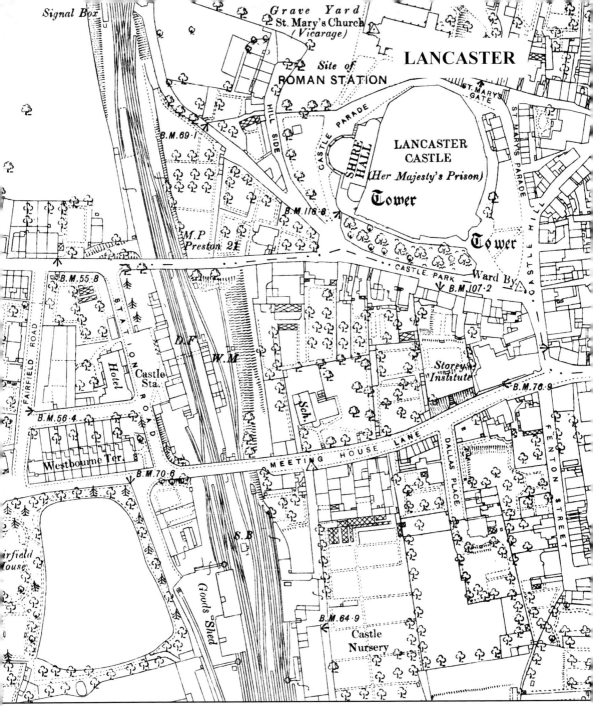

IIa & IIb *(opposite)*. Opened by the Lancaster & Carlisle Railway Company (L&CR) on 22nd September 1846, Lancaster Castle was the southern terminus of the route from Carlisle, although, as mentioned previously, the railway had intentions of reaching Preston. Map IIa of 1893, above, shows the original layout of Lancaster Castle station with two through lines. The main station building, located on the west (down) side, was designed by Sir William Tite in Tudor Revival style and, no, there was no earlier station regardless of the mention of 'Roman Station' on the map.

During the years 1900 to 1906 the station was remodelled significantly as seen in Map IIb, adjacent. A new entrance and ticket office were added to the east (up) side; again in Mock Tudor style with battlements mirroring Lancaster Castle above the station. The extensive remodelling gave rise to two bays on the west side of the station accommodated by platforms 1 and 2; four through main lines with platforms 3 and 4 accommodating the two outer lines. There were two further through lines passing through platforms 5 and 6, used generally by Midland Railway (MR) services to/from Morecambe and Heysham via Lancaster Green Ayre station. The line in platform 6 was electrified in 1908 for use by the Morecambe electrics; platform 5 followed suit in the 1950s. Both lines were de-energised in 1965 and overhead line equipment (OLE) removed in 1966. On 5th May 1969 the station was renamed 'Lancaster'. 1973 saw further rationalising of the lines with the little used track through platform 6 lifted.

In April 2022, the disused store rooms and offices in the Grade II listed building at the end of platforms 1 and 2 were turned into a pub named the Tite & Locke after the two men who played a key part in Lancaster's railway history.

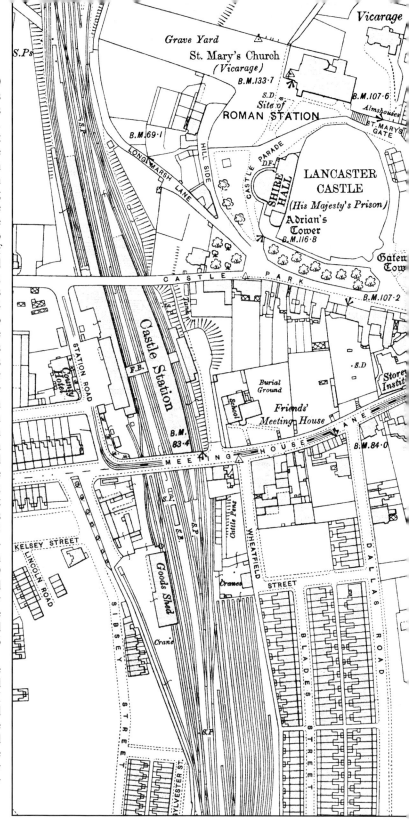

1. The main station building on the west side of the lines taken on 26th January 2023; it is notable that very little has changed since it was built. Why a replacement bus service when trains for Leeds were running in both directions? It transpired that the down platform at Wennington was taken out of use as the connecting footbridge was deemed defective. The bus service operated from Bentham, Wennington, Lancaster and Carnforth, while trains ran normally towards Wennington, Skipton and Leeds. Note the street entrance to the Tite & Locke pub on the left beyond the short-stay car park. (Mark Bartlett)

➔ *The zero milepost, located between platforms 4 and 5, was a 21 milepost until the early 1980s when it was changed. That would have been 21 miles from Preston rather than the distance from London. Why it was changed nobody seems to know. (Roy Davies)*

Other views of Lancaster can be found in Roy Davies' *Preston to Lancaster* **and** *Wennington to Morecambe and Heysham* **albums.**

2. A view of Lancaster Castle station looking south prior to its complete rebuilding, which took place between 1900 and 1906. MR coaches for the Morecambe branch can be seen in the bay on the left. Note how low the platforms were at that time. (Lens of Sutton Association, LOSA)

3. In this 1960s shot, Morecambe electric unit no. M28222M is seen arriving from Lancaster Green Ayre, having just climbed the steep gradient from the Midland main line. When the Morecambe line was re-energised in 1953, ex-LNWR units, previously employed on the London Euston to Watford services, were acquired; they were converted from fourth-rail DC electric stock in 1952 for use in Lancashire. Note the elaborate OLE steelwork; the LNWR insisted on such equipment rather than the wooden poles used mainly by the Midland. (Peter Fidczuk collection)

↑   4. The British Railways one-off GT3 4-6-0 approaches the station on the down main line working a 1Z79 test train on 2nd November 1961. BR Ivatt class 4 2-6-0 no. 43052 is seen standing alongside the goods warehouse waiting to depart with the driver looking on with interest no doubt. Built by English Electric in 1961, GT3 was the third prototype gas turbine locomotive; it was withdrawn in late 1962. Neither English Electric nor BR was prepared to fund further development of gas turbine technology as they were committed to diesel-electric locomotives. (Ron Herbert)

← 5. On 27th July 1962 ex-LMS Stanier Jubilee class 4-6-0 no. 45556 *Nova Scotia* arrives at Lancaster Castle with a Barrow to Manchester Victoria service. (Roger Joanes)

6. A summer 1963 shot of ex-LMS Stanier class 4MT 2-6-4T no. 42613 taking water at the north end of platform 3. To the left and right of the locomotive one can see the respective branches to Glasson Dock and Lancaster Green Ayre and No. 4 signal box in the background. (ColourRail.com/M.Chapman)

London & North Western Ry
Issued subject to the conditions & regulations in the Cos Time Tables Books Bills & Notices & unless stated therein to be so NOT available by Irish Mail
BURNESIDE TO
CARNFORTH (L.&N.W.)
VIA OXENHOLME
THIRD CLASS   624(S)   [Parly
CARNFORTH   FARE 1/5
2125
JA 1 04

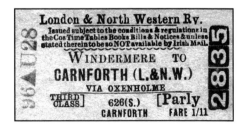

London & North Western Ry.
Issued subject to the conditions & regulations in the Cos Time Tables Books Bills & Notices & unless stated therein to be so NOT available by Irish Mail.
WINDERMERE TO
CARNFORTH (L.&N.W.)
VIA OXENHOLME
THIRD CLASS   626(S.)   [Parly
CARNFORTH   FARE 1/11
2835
96 AU 28

7. Ex-LMS Hughes/Fowler mixed traffic 2-6-0 no. 42878, known as a 'Crab' among the enthusiast fraternity, heads a freight from Preston through Lancaster. It is bound for Heysham Harbour on Saturday 20th June 1964. The well-dressed gentleman walking towards the camera on platform 3 is none other than Mr. Ron Herbert, a contributor to this album. Both Ron and fellow photographer, Noel, had rushed back from Glasson Dock to capture the last train from the small harbour. (Noel Machell)

8. BR Standard Britannia class 4-6-2 no. 70049 stands in platform 5 on 2nd August 1966. The locomotive is in a bit of a sorry state stripped of its *Solway Firth* nameplates. It is standing under the redundant steelwork that would have supported the OLE for the former Morecambe electrics. (ColourRail.com)

9. Two rather grimy Black 5s are seen at Lancaster on 8th July 1967. Ex-LMS Stanier Black 5 class 4-6-0 no. 45297 is standing at platform 3 with a Carlisle service and classmate no. 45294 is heading north on the through line. (Michael Ellis)

10. Black 5 no. 44680 is taking on water prior to departing with the 11.55 Euston - Carlisle service on 15th July 1967. Beyond the spotters is the former Lancaster No. 4 Signal Box, which had 144 levers. (Tom Heavyside)

11. A BR class 123 DMU stands at platform 2 on 21st May 1982. It was most probably on a Leeds - Morecambe service or return that required reversal at Lancaster. The units were the last first-generation DMUs built for British Railways at Swindon Works and designed like all Swindon units as inter-city sets. In terms of ride and comfort these units were far superior compared with the Pacers that followed. (Peter Smith)

12. BR class 31/4 also known as Brush Type 2 A1A-A1A no. 31408 is ready to depart with the 19.45 service to Hull on 11th August 1984. The locomotive was originally numbered D5646 and received its TOPS number in January 1974. (Tom Heavyside)

13. A seven-car APT test formation, led by driving trailer no. 370006 with central power cars nos 49006 and 49002, passes through Lancaster with the 1T26 15.55 Carlisle - Crewe test train on 7th October 1986. This was one of the last times an APT would pass through Lancaster as the project was formally abandoned not long after. An APT unit set the UK rail speed record of 162.2mph (261.0 km/h) in December 1979, which remains to this day on classic lines. The technology used in APTs was later sold to Fiat Ferroviaria and used for improving its second generation Pendolino trains, as used today in Avanti class 390 sets seen on the WCML. (Peter Smith)

14. Morecambe and Millom services wait in bay platforms 1 and 2 respectively on 1st September 2008. BR Pacer class 142 DMU no. 142093 is on the Morecambe run and BR class 156 two-car Super Sprinter no. 156454 is waiting to depart for Millom via Barrow-in-Furness. This shot was taken from the footpath that spans the station from Castle Park to Station Road. (Mark Bartlett)

↑ 15. A busy scene at Lancaster on 2nd December 2018. A class 144 Pacer departs platform 2 for Leeds, while an unidentified TransPennine Express Siemens Desiro design class 350 EMU arrives with a Manchester Airport service. In between, ex-Southern Railway Bulleid Merchant Navy class 4-6-2 no. 35018 *British India Line* waits in platform 3 with a 13-coach 'Santa Special' bound for Carlisle. This photo was taken from the same footbridge as in the previous picture. (Mark Bartlett)

16. The Spanish manufacturer CAF's 'Civity' class 195 no. 195118, operated by Northern Rail, has taken the down through line on 1st July 2019 on a Manchester Airport - Windermere service. A class 390 Pendolino is standing in platform 3 on a London Euston service. This was the first day of CAF Civity operations and the unit pictured was the first class 195 to traverse the Windermere branch in service. The class 156 Super Sprinters were used for a time on Windermere - Manchester Airport services but, with a maximum speed of 75mph (120kmh), struggled to keep time and some stops were omitted. When the 195s came in they ran initially to class 156 timings but, once fully in service, things began to speed up and stops were reintroduced. (Mark Bartlett)

17. The Tite & Locke pub is situated at the north end of platform 3, near platforms 1 and 2; it opened in April 2022 in a previously unused section of the Grade II listed building and consent was required before work started. The pub's name is a gesture to the two gentlemen who played such a pivotal role in Lancaster's railway history. (Mark Bartlett)

18. Viewed from the former platform 6 on 26th January 2023, BR class 158 DMU no. 158784 pulls into platform 5 on a Leeds - Morecambe service where it will reverse and continue on to Morecambe. Access to the former platform 6 is restricted and by appointment only. (Mark Bartlett)

Lune Crossing

III. Heading north out of Lancaster station this 1913 map shows the branches to Glasson Dock (left) and Green Ayre (right) then passing over St Georges Quay and the Lune via the Carlisle Bridge and the Midland line to Morecambe. Apart from remnants of the Green Ayre branch, all other lines are gone save the WCML that sweeps north heading towards Morecambe South Junction.

'Giant Axe Field' recreation ground, seen lower left, has been home to Lancaster City Football Club since 1911.

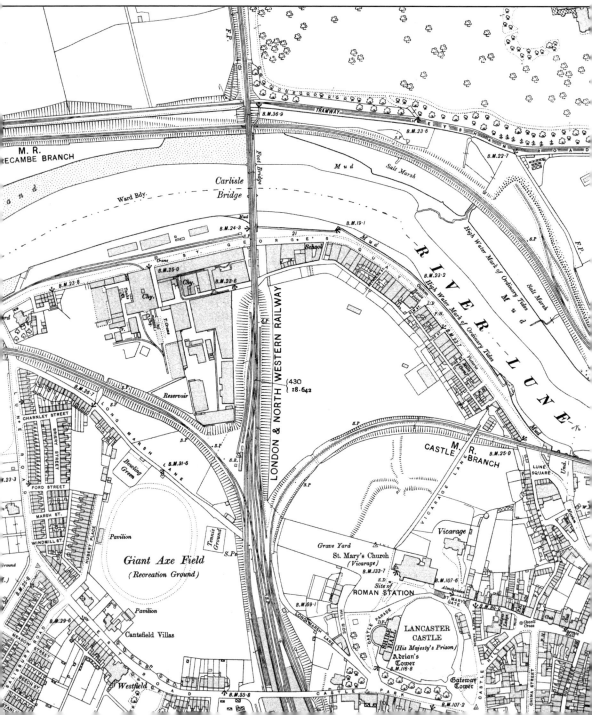

19. Ex-LMS Fowler/Stanier Royal Scot class 4-6-0 no. 46100 *Royal Scot* is seen on 4th March 2022 en route to the Keighley and Worth Valley Railway to attend the Spring Steam Gala. The scene appears to be a full train above St. George's Quay Road before crossing the Carlisle Bridge; in fact it was just the locomotive and support coach. (Will Smith)

← 20. On 28th April 2022 EMD class 66 Co-Co no. 66057 on the Seaforth - Mossend intermodal freight service is about to cross the Carlisle Bridge. Electro-Motive Diesel (EMD) was a division of General Motors when the 66s were built. In the background are the Castle and Priory. Lancaster Priory is the Church of England parish church of the City built on the site of a Benedictine priory dedicated to St Mary in 1094. Construction has continued throughout the centuries up to the 20th. The church and graveyard are listed as Grades I and II respectively. The Castle is a medieval fortress and former prison. It may have been founded in the 11th century on the site of a Roman fort overlooking the River Lune. (Will Smith)

21. Royal Scott class 4-6-0 no. 46100 *Royal Scot* glides across the Carlisle Bridge heading north out of Lancaster. It is hauling the 'Scot Commemorative' tour on Saturday 16th April 2016 from Crewe around the Cumbrian Coast to Carlisle. This locomotive was built in 1930 at Derby as no. 6152 *The King's Dragoon Guardsman* but in 1933, 6152 and 6100 swapped identities prior to the LMS sending a loco and train to the Century of Progress International Exposition in Chicago and no. 6100 was selected and travelled over 11,000 miles (17,600km) in the USA and Canada. Today no. 46100 carries a commemorative plaque below its nameplate recording its North American visit. No. 46100 is now owned by The Royal Scot Locomotive and General Trust and is based at Crewe. (Gordon Edgar)

Morecambe South Junction

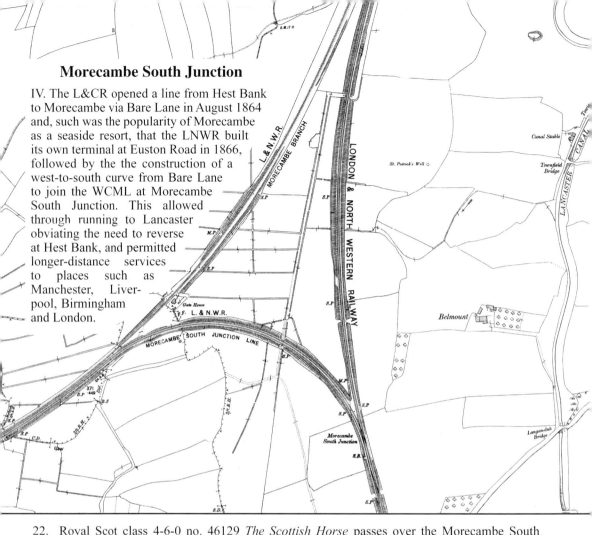

IV. The L&CR opened a line from Hest Bank to Morecambe via Bare Lane in August 1864 and, such was the popularity of Morecambe as a seaside resort, that the LNWR built its own terminal at Euston Road in 1866, followed by the the construction of a west-to-south curve from Bare Lane to join the WCML at Morecambe South Junction. This allowed through running to Lancaster obviating the need to reverse at Hest Bank, and permitted longer-distance services to places such as Manchester, Liverpool, Birmingham and London.

22.   Royal Scot class 4-6-0 no. 46129 *The Scottish Horse* passes over the Morecambe South Junction working 1L28 3.02pm north-bound Crewe to Workington Main on 3rd June 1961. The line diverging to the right leads to Bare Lane and Morecambe. (Ron Herbert)

BARE LANE

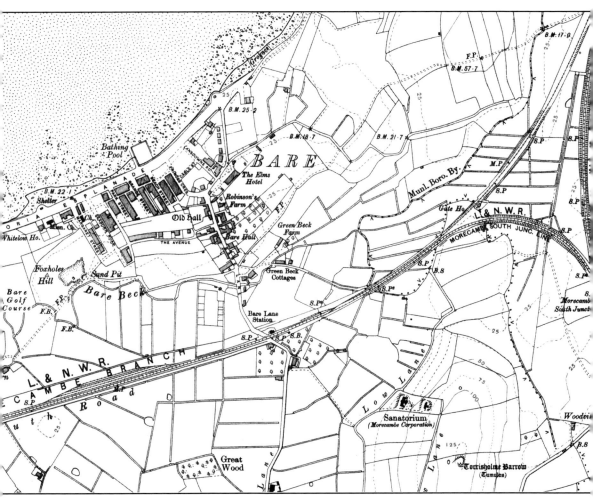

V. Opened by the LNWR on 8th August 1864 as Poulton-le-Sands, the station was renamed 'Bare Lane' a few months later, on 31st October. Bare Lane is the road that crosses the line immediately to the west of the station as seen in this 1919 extract, derived from a 6in to 1 mile map. The station has undergone several changes:

[1] the signal box was taken out of use in December 1994 but remained on site for another year as a passenger information office and;

[2] the former station building, now in private hands, was featured in the BBC's *Homes Under the Hammer* series.

To today's casual visitors the station is standard double-track with two platforms but all is not what it seems. To the east of Bare Lane the lines from the north curve and south junction converge then immediately diverge into two separate bi-directional running lines. The line next to platform 1 is effectively a long siding that runs into the bay platform at Morecambe; whereas, the line through platform 2 enables trains to reach Heysham Port by reversing at Morecambe - see map VI, overleaf.

Bare Lane station benefits from an active volunteer group that maintains the station environment for the local community, visitors and passengers. Children at a nearby school are sponsored by the adopters to plant flowers and vegetables in and around the station.

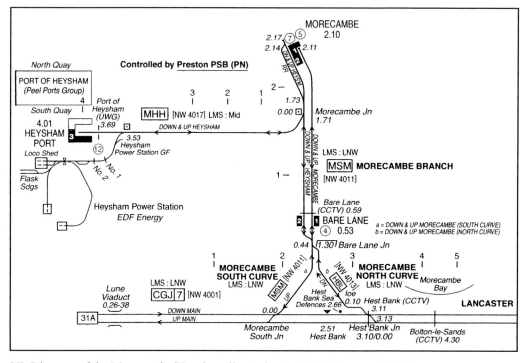

VI. Diagram of the Morecambe/Heysham line today. (©TRACKmaps, 2018)

↗ 23. In this undated photograph a train is about to depart for Morecambe. While undated it was certainly before the crossing keeper's hut was replaced by the signal box in 1937. (John Alsop collection)

→ 24. On Sunday evenings during the summer season there were a number of returning day excursion trains from Morecambe Euston Road station to various destinations in the Lancashire industrial areas and here we see Black 5 4-6-0 no. 45441 working the 8.00pm special to Colne in northeast Lancashire on 12th July 1959. Awaiting the passage of the train is a lady on her 'Rudge' bicycle and Ribble Motor Services no. 2776 on the L14 service from Bare to Lancaster. Unlike the passing train, the crew outnumber the sole passenger by a ratio of 2 to 1. The Balloon Sidings can be seen to the right of the foreground concrete lamp post; the sidings were used during busy times for storing rolling stock from excursion trains. (Noel Machell)

25. Ex-LMS Fowler class 4F 0-6-0 no. 44041 is working the 11.21 Morecambe Promenade to Carnforth local freight on 24th August 1961. The Bare Lane coal merchant's loaded wagon is marshalled next to the engine ready to be detached into the goods siding alongside platform 1. Here we see the early turn signalman, the late Dennis Parkinson, having just given the fireman the single line token for permission to proceed on to the single line to Hest Bank. In 1963 the coal siding, connection to the up main line and all applicable signals were removed. (Ron Herbert)

LANCASTER and MORECAMBE.—L. M. & S.

Down. — Week Days.

Miles	Castle Station,	mrn	mrn		mrn	mrn		mrn	mrn	mrn	non	aft	aft	aft	aft	aft	aft	aft	aft	aft	aft	aft
	Lancaster.........dep.	7 20	8 0	....	....	9 10	....	9 40	....	1110	12 0	1220	1240	1 15	1 45	2 20	2 45	3 20	3 43	4 20	5 10	5 53	6 36
2¾	Bare Lane...:	7 26	8 6	....	8 38	9 16	....	9 46	1054	1116	12 6	1226	1246	1 21	1 51	2 26	2 51	3 26	4 0	4 26	5 16	5 59	6 42
4	Morecambe (Eus. Rd) ar.	7 30	8 10	....	8 42	9 20	....	9 50	1057	1120	1210	1230	1250	1 25	1 55	2 30	2 55	3 30	4 5	4 30	5 20	6 3	6 46

Down. — Week Days—Continued. / Sundays.

Castle Station,	aft	aft	aft	aft	aft			mrn	mrn	aft	aft	aft	aft	aft	aft	aft	aft	aft	aft
Lancaster.........dep.	7 15	8 15	9 50	10 5	1050	....	....	9 10	1145	2 25	....	....	4 30	5 0	5 30	....	6 20	7 0	8	9 0	9 50	....
Bare Lane.............	7 21	8 21	9 56	1011	1056	....	....	9 16	1151	2 31	2 42	4 17	4 36	5 6	5 36	6 17	6 26	7 6	8 9	6 9 56	....
Morecambe (Eus. Rd.)..arr.	7 25	8 25	10 0	1015	11 0	....	....	9 20	1155	2 35	2 45	4 20	4 40	5 10	5 40	6 20	6 30	7 10	8 10	9 10 10 9	....

Up. — Week Days.

Miles	Euston Road,	mrn	mrn	mrn	mrn	mrn	mrn	mrn	mrn	mrn	mrn	non		aft	aft	aft	aft	aft	aft	aft	aft	aft
	Morecambe.......dep.	6 35	7 25	8 0	8 15	8 30	9 10	9 15	10 5	1010	1120	12 0	....	1220	1 20	1 55	3 15	4 15	5 20	5 40	6 30	7 35	8 20
1¼	Bare Lane....[323, 334	6 37	7 27	2 8	17 8	32 9	12 9	17 10	7 10	12 1122	12 2	....	1222	1 22	1 57	3 17	4 17	5 22	5 42	6 32	7 37	8 22
4	Lancaster (Castle) ††arr.	6 45	7 35	8 10	8 25	8 40	....	9 25	1015	1026	1130	1210	....	....	1 30	2 5	3 25	4 25	5 30	....	6 40	7 45	8 30

Up. — Week Days—Continued. / Sundays.

Euston Road,	aft	aft	aft	aft	aft	aft		mrn	aft	aft	aft	aft	aft	aft	aft	aft	aft	aft	aft	aft	aft
Morecambe............dep.	9 15	9 35	1015	1030	1040	1110	....	9 30	1 15	2 45	3 0	4 30	4 50	5 30	5 50	6 40	7	0 7	25	7 30	8 30	9 30	1010
Bare Lane........[323, 334	9 17	9 37	1017	1032	1042	1112	....	9 32	1 17	2 47	3 2	4 32	4 52	5 32	5 52	6 42	7	2 7	27	7 32	8 32	9 32	1012
Lancaster (Castle) †† arr.	9 25	9 45	1025	....	1050	1120	....	....	1 25	....	3 10	4 40	5 0	....	6	0 6	50	7 10	....	7 40	8 40	9 40	1020

C. Wednesdays and Saturdays.
E. Except Saturdays.
S. Saturdays only.
U. Mondays and Saturdays.

V. Except Mondays and Saturdays.
X. One class only.

†† About ¾ mile to Green Ayre.

☞ **For other Trains**

July 1924

26. On 15th July 1967 Carnforth-based Black 5 no. 44948 is seen hauling the Summer Saturday-only Glasgow - Morecambe service. The locomotive had taken over from a pair of class 37 diesel locomotives at Carlisle, from where the photographer had travelled on the train as far as Bare Lane. The previous week the driver of Britannia no. 70045 *Lord Rowallan* reportedly forgot to stop at Bare Lane. The photographer is proud of the fact that this image is displayed on one of the community noticeboards at the station. Black 5 no. 44948 was withdrawn from service less than three months after this shot was taken. (Michael Ellis)

27. Peaks were unusual motive power in north Lancashire, so, when BR class 46 1Co-Co1 no. 46029 turned up on the SO 09.28 Leeds - Morecambe working, on 3rd August 1980, it was indeed a rare occurrence. No. 46029 is seen here with the return working the 11.45 SO Morecambe - Leeds service, running into Bare Lane. The stock for the trip was made up of Western Region carriages off the 18.30 FO Penzance - Leeds working; so it could be loosely claimed to have been a Penzance - Morecambe service. On 8th December 2012 the signal box was closed and the lines came under the control of Preston power box. (Peter Smith)

28. Stadler Rail and previously Vossloh España class 68 diesel electric Bo-Bo locomotives are in charge of a nuclear flask train on 30th September 2021. No. 68001 *Evolution* leads, with no. 68033 bringing up the rear; the train is seen having passed Bare Lane en route to Heysham Power Station. The train will reverse at Morecambe and take the Heysham Branch. Heysham no. 1 Power Station will cease generating in 2024 while Heysham 2 will continue into the 2030s. (Mark Bartlett)

29. Based at Derby, the one-off BR class 950 DMU no. 950001, modelled on class 150/1 Sprinters and operated by Network Rail, was purpose-built for track assessment rather than carrying passengers. On 28th May 2015 it visited the Morecambe and Heysham branches while on a circuit of the north-west. That same day it had travelled to Windermere, Hellifield, Blackburn and the Preston Dock branch. The unit is seen here en route to Carnforth at the end of the day's operation. (Mark Bartlett)

Balloon Sidings

Located just to the west of Bare Lane station the Balloon Sidings were used for storing empty coaching stock associated with the numerous excursions to Morecambe - see map V. Today the sidings are long gone and the site is occupied by houses on Grasmere Road.

30.   Black 5 no. 44758 is with an unidentified up passenger service passing the Balloon Sidings in July 1964. Some of the damaged stock from the 1965 Hest Bank accident were stored temporarily in the sidings. (Cumbrian Railway Association/Pearsall collection)

31. This shot was taken on 7th July 1967 when Black 5 no. 45445 was shunting ex-LMS stock and several coaches became derailed. The photographer happened, at the time, to be in a house that backed on to the Balloon Sidings and heard a loud clunk and this was the outcome. (Michael Ellis)

32. Ex-LMS Stanier class 8F 2-8-0 no. 48081 brought the breakdown crane from Carnforth to attend. The sidings are long gone and are home to a number of bungalows. (Michael Ellis)

London & North Western Ry.
Issued subject to the conditions & regulations in
the Coy Time Tables Books Bills & Notices.
CHILD
HEST BANK TO
LANCASTER (CASTLE) (LNW)
THIRD
CLASS
REVISED
FARE -/2½
8 JE '25
972

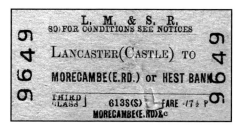

L. M. & S. R.
SO) FOR CONDITIONS SEE NOTICES
LANCASTER (CASTLE) TO
MORECAMBE (E.RD.) or HEST BANK
THIRD
CLASS
613S(S)   FARE -/7½ P
MORECAMBE(E.RD)&c
9649

POULTON LANE

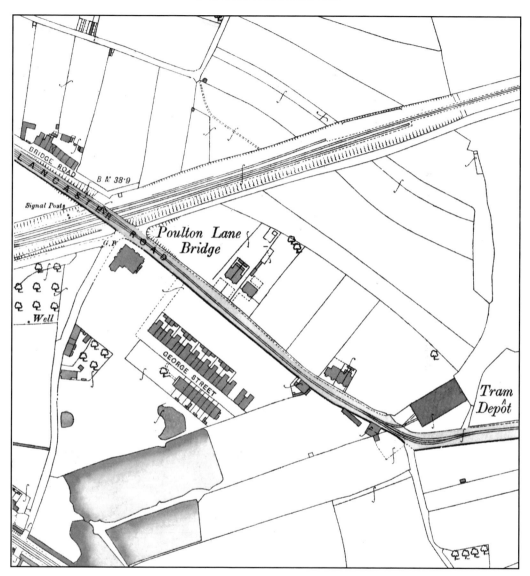

VII. Initially the L&CR shared the MR Morecambe station at Northumberland Street but, due to congestion, was obliged to open its own station at Poulton Lane, which it did on 8th August 1864. By then the growth in visitors to the resort had been dramatic. Sadly there are no known photographs of the station and the maps give scant information, as seen above. Even the name 'Poulton Lane' is confusing as even the oldest published maps show Lancaster Road crossing the line, although reference is made to Poulton Lane Bridge. Perhaps Lancaster Road was called Poulton Lane before the arrival of tram services to Lancaster. The station was to the east of the Lancaster Road bridge. In 1886 the LNWR built a larger station at Euston Road and on 9th May 1886, the day before it opened, Poulton Lane station closed for good. It is noteworthy to mention that Morecambe was also linked to Lancaster by tram with the local depot prominent on this map.

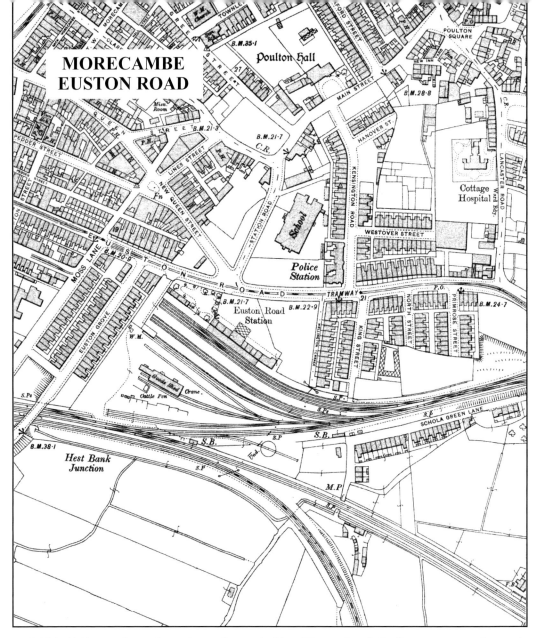

VIII. This 1913 map shows the station to the south side of Euston Road. Earlier, entrance to the goods yard was by way of the Morecambe Promenade line only. Here it is shown having access from both lines. The whole passenger station complex has gone and is replaced by retirement flats and other buildings. The goods yard is now a builders' merchant and includes the former goods shed.

In 1965 BR was granted an Act of Parliament to construct a new spur just to the east of Euston Road station to the former Midland Heysham branch. The new line would enable complete closure of the Midland line between Lancaster and Morecambe and allow trains to run to Heysham without having to reverse at Morecambe Promenade. Under the plan, Promenade station was to close and Euston Road would either be rebuilt or repositioned on the alignment of the new link. The new line would have required demolition of some houses along its route.

The plan never came to fruition and, to this day, Heyham-bound trains are still required to reverse at Morecambe.

33.   The station was opened by the LNWR on 9th May 1886 simply as Morecambe, which was typical of railway companies at the time even though there was another station of the same name in the town. Following the 1923 grouping, the LMS added the suffix 'Euston Road' to the name. Constructed mainly of yellow brick it was rather an elaborate affair for what was the terminus of a branch line, although it did come into its own during the summers when tourists and holiday-makers flocked to the resort. This shot was taken on 31st December 1965 some time after the station closed to passengers, although the car park was still operating with charges payable at the kiosk. (Colour.Rail.com/J Tolson)

34.   In this undated photo, an LNWR 2-4-2T has just arrived at Euston Road with a healthy number of passengers. Compared with Promenade station, Euston Road was always less busy and even more so when the London Midland Region transferred winter schedule passenger services to Promenade station from 15th September 1958. (LOSA)

→ 35. BR Ivatt class 4MT 2-6-0 no. 43117 shunts the stock at platform 1 in readiness for the 11.48am Euston Road to Lancaster Castle on 7th September 1961. Ron Herbert's father, Arthur, became station master in 1959 and his sister, Pat, had a Saturday job as the station announcer on summer Saturdays in the late 1950s. Euston Road signal box, seen on the left, opened on 12th May 1891 and closed on 26th November 1967. Also in view are the former electrified Midland lines from Lancaster Green Ayre and Heysham on the left, not to mention the roller coaster in the background that stood in the fairground. (Ron Herbert)

↓ 36. Ivatt no. 43117 is now ready to depart with the aforementioned service to Lancaster Castle. With 7th September 1961 being a Thursday, it corrects statements made by some that the station was only open on summer Saturdays in that year. The last passenger service out of Euston Road was the 4.25pm service to Lancaster Castle on 8th September 1962. Thereafter it was used to stable coaching stock, when the need arose, and was used also for marshalling and sorting parcels during the Christmas period until 1963. (Ron Herbert)

37. A deserted station, save for empty coaching stock, on 31st December 1965.
(ColourRail.com/J. Tolson)

38. Bereft of track, the platforms were taken out of use on 16th April 1967 but the station buildings were still intact as seen on 5th May 1968. This situation may have been due to the plans passed in 1965 to build the spur to the Heysham branch. The decision not to build it in effect determined the former station's fate. The site was demolished in the late 1970s giving way to the retirement flats we see today. The goods yard continued in operation until 9th October 1972. (John Alsop collection)

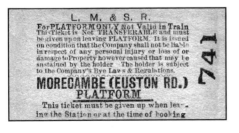

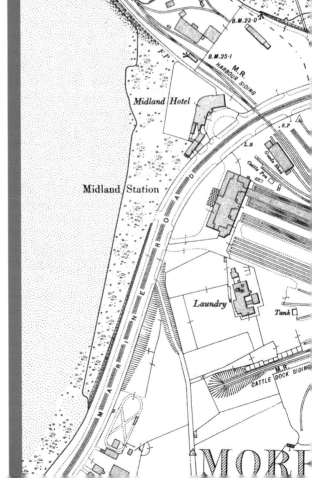

MORECAMBE PROMENADE

IX. This 1913 map shows the extensive facilities associated with Morecambe Promenade station, which opened on 24th March 1907 simply as Morecambe. It was positioned opposite the old Midland Hotel after being relocated to the west by a few hundred yards from the original site at the end of Northumberland Street. Much of the terminus frontage had been constructed from brickwork removed from the former station.

On 2nd June 1924 the station was renamed Morecambe Promenade, to avoid confusion with Euston Road station, but reverted to Morecambe on 6th May 1968. While Morecambe Harbour station closed on 1st September 1904, trains continued to serve the jetty until the late 1920s, which then saw the line severed with the opening of the new Midland Hotel in 1933. From September 1962 all trains serving the former LNWR branch transferred to Promenade station with the closure of Euston Road to passengers. With final closure of the former Midland route to Morecambe in 1967, all traffic to Morecambe and Heysham ran via Bare Lane with all traffic to Heysham Harbour required to reverse at Morecambe, which is still the case today.

The station closed on 7th February 1994 with bus transfers to Bare Lane and Lancaster until the present station opened on 29th May 1994. After closure, all evidence of track work was lost under Morecambe Market and the neighbouring retail park but the terminal building remained as a live entertainment venue known as The Platform. However, its long-term future is now under threat as part of the local council's cost-cutting exercise.

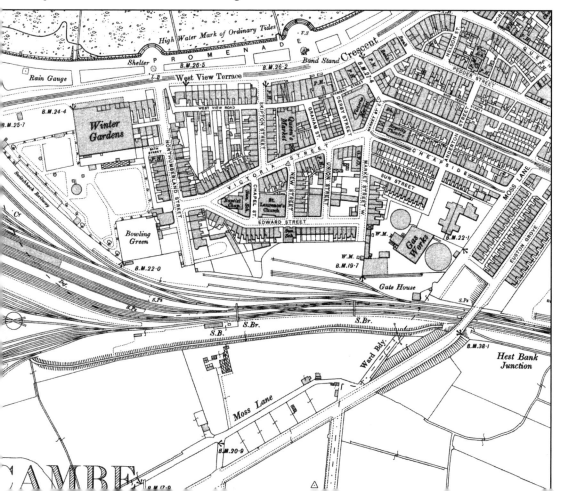

39. This photo was taken on 25th May 1977, some nine years after reverting simply to Morecambe and 17 years before closure. (ColourRail.com/D.L. Dott)

40. Black 5 no. 44904 is with a service most likely bound for Lancaster Castle in July 1963. (ColourRail.com)

MORECAMBE

41. A shot of Morecambe station taken on 15th January 2023. The ticket office is staffed by Northern Rail from Monday to Saturday, 07.45 until 14.45. The entrance flower bed on the left is awaiting planting but will the Community Station Adopters sow wildflower seeds as they did in 2022. (David A. Alexander)

42. Platforms 1 and 2 after a snow fall on 9th December 2022. To the right of the line at platform 2 is the passing loop that is now little used as nuclear flask trains are top and tailed, obviating the need to run around at Morecambe. (Michael Ellis)

RAILWAY DEVELOPMENT AT MORECAMBE

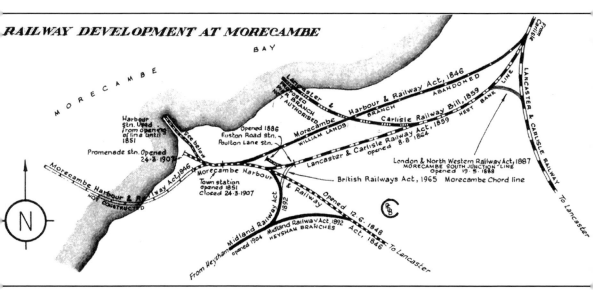

X. The route north to Hest Bank is taken via the Morecambe Branch Line (north curve) - see map V. Back in the day, William Lands had other ideas; he proposed under an Act of 1846 a more direct line to Morecambe from Hest Bank. However the L&CR branch from Hest Bank held sway and Lands' idea was abandoned as was the spur to Morecambe pier. Apparently there are still some earthworks at Hest Bank marking the start of the Lands branch. This sketch map shows also the proposed direct route from near Morecambe Euston Road to the Heysham Harbour branch referred to in the notes to map V. When opened in 1864 the L&CR Morecambe branch was double-track but later singled when the South Curve to the WCML was constructed in 1888 to cope with ever-increasing holiday traffic.
(Sketch map, *The Midland Railway North of Leeds*, Peter E. Baughan)

➜ 43. Metro-Vick Co-Bo D5716 passes the outer home signal for Bare Lane Junction on Sunday 24th March 1963 as it proceeds along the single line spur from Hest Bank. The train, which is being diverted via Morecambe Promenade (reversal) and Lancaster Green Ayre (reversal), is the 10.53am departure from Workington bound for London Euston; the diesel locomotive will be detached at Preston. Note the corrugated signal arm and substantial timber post, the West Coast main line is just visible to the right of D5716 at marker light level. (Noel Machell)

➜ 44. On 3rd August 1967 Black 5 no. 45092 hauls a mixed freight away from Hest Bank on the Morecambe branch bound for Heysham Harbour. Note the brake van behind the locomotive; this is in place according to running rules regarding reversal at Morecambe Promenade station for the onward trip to Heysham. (Tom Heavyside)

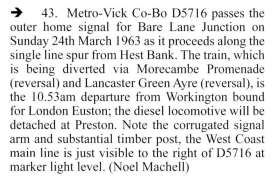

45. It does not take four mainline diesel locomotives to haul two nuclear flasks, so it is likely that the spare diesels were hitching a lift to Sellafield instead of returning light engine. In this shot, taken in August 2012, Direct Rail Services class 37/6 nos 37604 and 37602, BR class 47 Brush Type 4 no. 47802 and BR class 20/3 English Electric Type 1 no. 20309 are heading north approaching the level crossing. Class 47 47802 is now in the West Coast Railways fleet based at Carnforth. (Cameron Seddon)

46. BR class 90 25 kV AC Bo-Bo locomotive no. 90021, in Malcolm Rail livery, and a sister locomotive, double-head a Daventry - Grangemouth intermodal freight passing the site of Hest Bank station on 21st January 2023. Although known as the West Coast Main Line this is the only location on the route between London and Glasgow where it comes close to the west coast. (Will Gibson)

HEST BANK

XI. This 1913 map shows the layout at Hest Bank station that changed little until 1969 when the camping coaches that occupied the former goods yard were removed. Nothing remains of the station today and the Morecambe branch was extended north and follows the line of one of the former platforms as part of the WCML 1973 electrification programme. The station was opened by the L&CR on 22nd September 1846 and was closed on 3rd February 1969. The signal box, now disused, remained in operation to control the level crossings at Hest Bank and Bolton-le-Sands a little further north. In May 2013 both crossings came under the control of Preston Power Box.

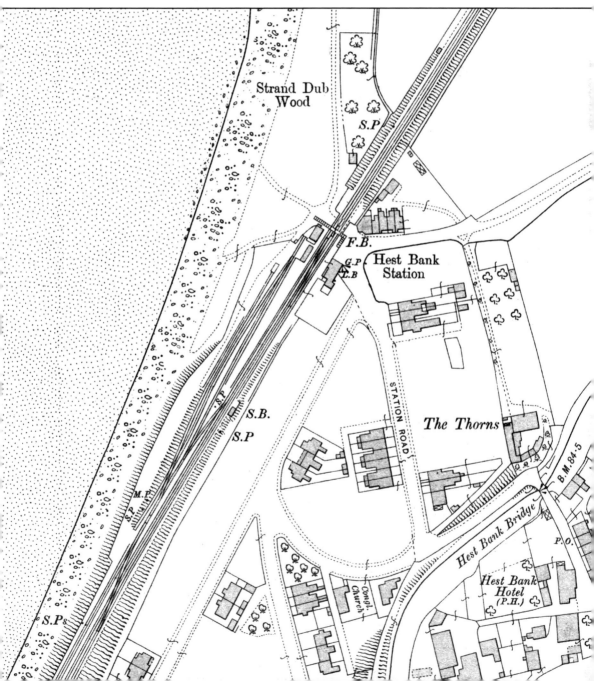

47. An LNWR steam railcar seen at Hest Bank circa 1923. Six railcars were built between 1905 and 1907 and all passed into LMS service in 1923. One, no. 3, was withdrawn in 1948 having been out of service since an accident in 1947. (Robert Humm collection)

48. Clearing up at Hest Bank after the 1V42 22.10 Glasgow - Kensington Olympia sleeper was partially derailed early on 20th May 1965 by a broken rail just north of the station. The nine rear coaches were derailed but not BR Brush/Sulzer Type 4 no. D1633 and the first three coaches. Mercifully there were no fatalities and only 11 minor injuries. (Andrewstransport)

49. On 27th July 1965, some weeks after the accident, Lostock Hall steam crane (left) and Carlisle Kingmoor steam crane (right) were in the process of making the remainder of the derailed vehicles fit to travel to Morecambe Balloon sidings. The steam cranes arrived soon after the accident to clear the main lines of derailed vehicles to allow single line working to be introduced; unlike today the aim was to get trains moving again and not close the line as a potential crime scene.

The sleeping cars off 1V42 can be seen stabled in the former bay platform with the resident camping coaches in the background. The photographer's father was the station master at the time but he, Ron Herbert and a friend were chasing steam between Calais and Amiens when the derailment took place and only became aware of it when they returned to Folkestone. There were no mobiles in 1965. (Ron Herbert)

50. BR Britannia no. 70010 *Owen Glendower* heads a down parcels service from Lancaster on 3rd August 1967. The rather scruffy looking engine is missing its nameplates but those with a keen eye will see the name painted on the smoke deflector. It was withdrawn from service in the following September. The camping coaches were a familiar sight having occupied the former goods yard since it closed on 2nd December 1963 until the end of the 1969 season, although the station closed in February of that year. (Tom Heavyside)

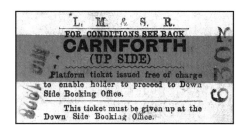

L. M. & S. R.
FOR CONDITIONS SEE BACK
CARNFORTH
(UP SIDE)
Platform ticket issued free of charge
to enable holder to proceed to Down
Side Booking Office.
This ticket must be given up at the
Down Side Booking Office.

London & North Western Ry.
Issued subject to the conditions & regulations in
the Coa Time Tables Books Bills & Notices & unless
stated therein to be so NOT available by Irish Mail.
BOLTON-LE-SANDS TO
HEST BANK
THIRD CLASS   618(S.)   [Parly
HEST BANK   FARE -/1½

51. Black 5 no. 45193 passes the level crossing in the summer of 1967 while a Ford Anglia De Luxe waits for the gates to open. (ColourRail.com)

52. BR class 37/7 Co-Co no. 37704 (formerly D6704 and later 37034) is seen in EWS livery on the up main line, just north of the level crossing, while engineering work was being carried out on 26th January 2002. (Gary Lewis)

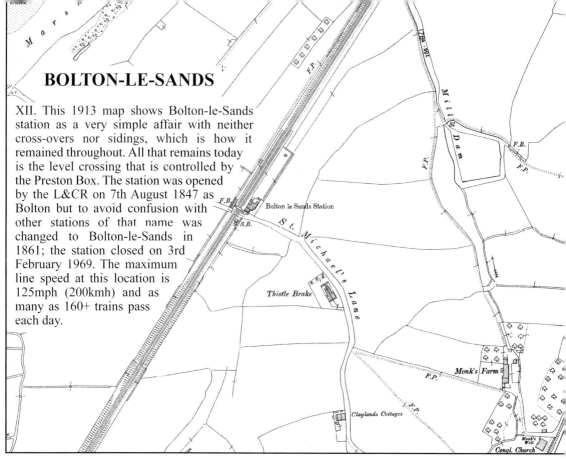

BOLTON-LE-SANDS

XII. This 1913 map shows Bolton-le-Sands station as a very simple affair with neither cross-overs nor sidings, which is how it remained throughout. All that remains today is the level crossing that is controlled by the Preston Box. The station was opened by the L&CR on 7th August 1847 as Bolton but to avoid confusion with other stations of that name was changed to Bolton-le-Sands in 1861; the station closed on 3rd February 1969. The maximum line speed at this location is 125mph (200kmh) and as many as 160+ trains pass each day.

Bolton le Sands Station

Thistle Brake

St. Michael's Lane

Monk's Farm

Claylands Cottages

Congl. Church

53. The signal seen in the shot was very common on the Preston & Lancaster Junction Railway and the L&CR dating from about 1840-50. They were from the era of time interval working with one arm for each direction. Angled down they are clear and horizontal meant stop; they were worked from levers at the base of the post. They were usually located close to the points, junctions or stations they were to protect and there would be a fixed Distant called Auxiliary signals at the time at least 200 yards away to warn of its location. Normally, five minutes after a train departing it would be cleared; hence the importance of a guard to protect the train if it failed in a section. This was because another train could follow as demonstrated by the Bay Horse accidents of 21st August 1848 and 24th October 1861. It is an interesting photo because it shows telegraph poles; so it was quite possible the early form of telegraph block working was in place at the time. (LOSA)

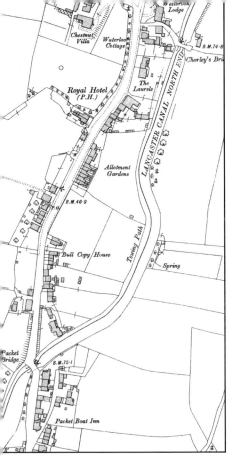

54. On 21st July 1958 the 6.10pm goods train from Carnforth to Lancaster is hauled by ex-LMS Fowler 3F 0-6-0T no. 47339, passing some eight minutes later through the rural wayside station. Punctuality of this train was important as it was followed by the 3.00pm Glasgow Central to Euston and the 4.40pm Carlisle to London Broad Street meat train in quick succession. (Noel Machell)

55. GB Railfreight no. 66735 *Peterborough United* heads north past Bolton-le-Sands on 29th September 2019 with a very unusual load of Foxhound protected patrol vehicles. This train was a very rare movement from Warminster to Elgin for the Ministry of Defence. (Andrewstransport)

South of Carnforth - Crag Bank

56. This shot taken on 9th June 1965 shows the southern approach to the busy Carnforth railway complex with the station ahead and motive power depot to the left. Class 8F 2-8-0 no. 48039 is seen heading an up empty stock working off the Furness line passing Black 5 no. 44874 hauling a down freight. (Robert Humm collection)

57. Past and present shots often show a forlorn image of today compared with the past but that cannot be said about Carnforth, as any enthusiast or passenger will testify. On 27th April 2022 Avanti Pendolino no. 390046 speeds past the Carnforth loops at Crag Bank on a northbound service; while on the far left two Jubilees no. 45596 *Bahamas* and no. 45690 *Leander* on the 'GB XIV' rail tour are being watered before continuing to Chester. In between is a BR class 158 Express Sprinter DMU no. 158867 that had just arrived from Skipton on a service terminating at Carnforth. It later went forward to Lancaster as empty stock. (Mark Bartlett)

CARNFORTH

58. Not the most imposing frontage for a station at such an important railway centre. Since this shot was taken, on 8th February 1999, some of the former offices have been let to various retail outlets, including the Snug Micro Pub that opened on 12th September 2012. (ColourRail.com/L. McEwan)

59. A view of the south end of Carnforth station circa 1900. Note the chimney marking the location of the ironworks. (Robert Humm collection)

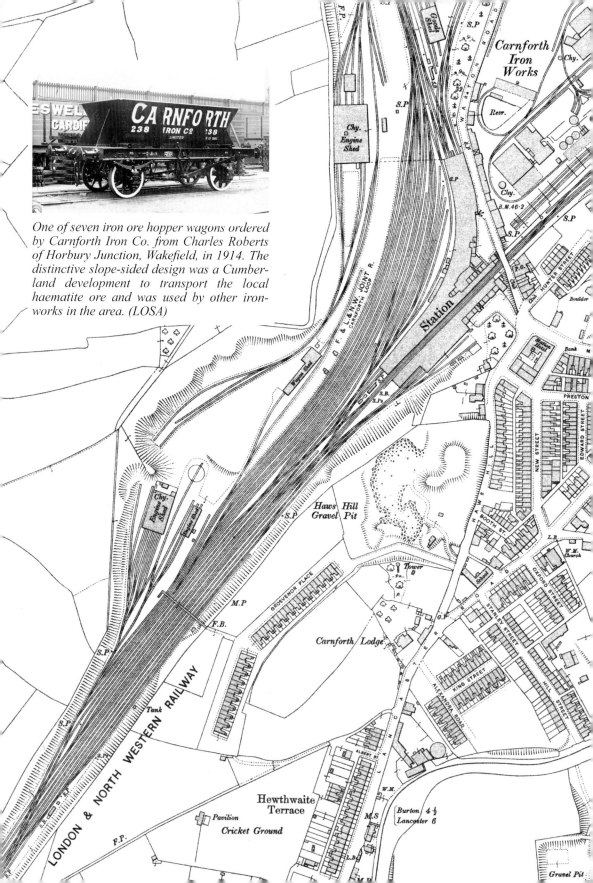

One of seven iron ore hopper wagons ordered by Carnforth Iron Co. from Charles Roberts of Horbury Junction, Wakefield, in 1914. The distinctive slope-sided design was a Cumberland development to transport the local haematite ore and was used by other ironworks in the area. (LOSA)

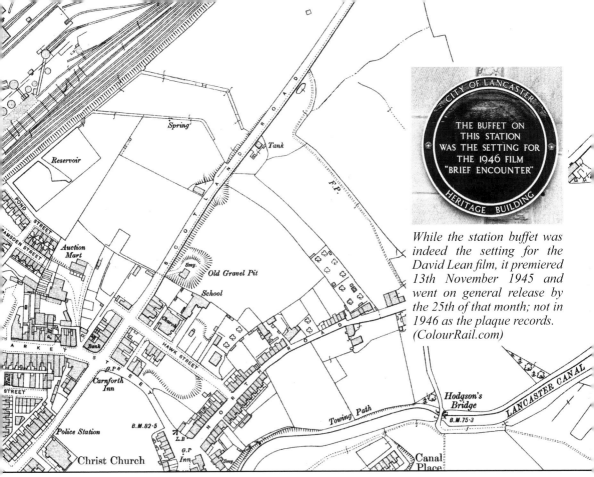

While the station buffet was indeed the setting for the David Lean film, it premiered 13th November 1945 and went on general release by the 25th of that month; not in 1946 as the plaque records. (ColourRail.com)

XIII. Situated some 7 miles (11.2kms) north of Lancaster, the market town of Carnforth grew during the the latter part of the 1800s as a result of the ironworks and burgeoning railway. The L&CR opened a station in 1846 and, in 1857, it served as a terminus for the Ulverston & Lancaster Railway that was absorbed in 1862 by the Furness Railway. Later, the MR came to Carnforth by way of the Furness & Midland Joint Railway and Carnforth emerged from what was not much more than a wayside halt, initially, to a much larger station. This served a three-way junction and three major railway companies. In 1846 the Carnforth Ironworks Company was established near the station and was connected to the network by a tramway. The ironworks continued production until 1929 when the site was taken over by the War Department as an ordnance depot; that lasted until the 1960s and the site is now home to an industrial estate.

As well as the station being enlarged in the latter part of the 19th century the site was also home to locomotive sheds serving the three companies. In addition, the LNWR opened a wagon repair shop on site around 1903, which was later modernised by the LMS in 1923. The building has remained in use ever since and now houses a facility for repairing historic rolling stock. The outbreak of World War II saw increasing pressure on industries and the railways in the northwest as they were beyond the range of German bombers; so much so, that the Government agreed to fund construction of a new Motive Power Depot that opened in 1944.

Following the end of steam, much of the site to the west of the running lines became the visitor attraction, Steamtown Carnforth, named after Steamtown in the USA, a mecca for steam enthusiasts far and wide. It became home to a number of famous locomotives including the *Flying Scotsman*. Lack of investment heralded Steamtown's decline in the 1990s but all was not lost as West Coast Railways (WCR) came to the rescue. Apart from occasional open days the museum and visitor attraction are no longer open to the public. In effect, WCR operates a working railway depot with extensive repair and maintenance facilities and is home to steam and diesel hauled trains that operate across the national railway network. Last but not least, platform 1 of Carnforth station is home to the Heritage Centre that featured in David Lean's classic film, *Brief Encounter*, starring Celia Johnson and Trevor Howard.

60. A view from under the canopy looking north from the south end of the platforms on 29th May 1906. The Furness Railway up platform is on the left and the LNWR down platform is to the right. The subway to the exit is between them with the *Brief Encounter* clock over the entrance. (LOSA)

61. Black 5 no. 44897 is about to depart platform 1 on 25th August 1967; no. 44897 was a Carnforth-based locomotive. (ColourRail.com)

62.   WCML platforms 1 and 2 were closed in May 1970, following the withdrawal of local stopping passenger services between Lancaster and Carlisle two years earlier. This southerly view was captured in February 1972. It shows the platforms before the walls facing the fast lines were demolished, cut back and fenced off, prior to the commissioning of 25 kV overhead electrification in 1974. (ColourRail.com/J. Richardson)

63. Alstom class 67 Bo-Bo diesel electric loco no. 67005 *Queen's Messenger*, in purple livery with red lining, heads the Royal Train northwards en route to Oxenholme on 9th April 2014. It was conveying the then HRH Prince of Wales on a visit to Cumbria. No. 67005 was one of the 30 67s leased to DB Cargo UK and used primarily as class 47 replacements for hauling high-speed Royal Mail and passenger trains. The Waiting Room is the one featured in *Brief Encounter*. (Mark Bartlett)

Carnforth Motive Power Depot

64. Carnforth MPD was built on the site of the old LNWR depot by Italian prisoners of war in 1944 and replaced three former depots: the Furness Railway shed that was demolished in 1938-39 followed by the LNWR shed a few years later. The MR shed to the east of the WCML was retained as a warehouse. On Saturday 2nd July 1966, photographer, Ron Herbert, climbed to the top of the coaling plant carrying two cameras to take this shot. The locomotives in view are:

Class 5 nos 44733 and 45054, ex-LMS Ivatt class 4MT 2-6-0 nos 43066, 43095 and 43103, and a further class 5 no. 45328 below, under the ash plant. Interestingly all these engines were allocated to Carnforth shed code 10A. Also in the photograph is an English Electric Type 4 class 40 and two BR class 08 0-6-0 350hp shunters. The six-road shed had a wheel drop, workshop and forge, a 70ft (21m) turntable plus a 150 ton (152 tonnes) capacity coaling plant capable of loading four locomotives in 10 minutes and a recycling ash plant alongside. (Ron Herbert)

65. This undated shot of the MPD looks south with class 08 shunters on duty as well as steam on shed. (ColourRail.com)

66. Taken on 25th November 1967 looking south from the shed itself. Black 5 no. 45342 is in the centre with another unidentified Black 5, on the left, and a Carnforth-based BR class 4 4-6-0 moving away on the right. (John Hunt)

67. These were to be the final gasps of Britannia 4-6-2 no. 70021 without its *Morning Star* name plates. In steam at Carnforth, on Saturday 30th December 1967, it didn't have a home to go to; its home shed, Carlisle Kingmoor, was to eradicate steam traction at midnight on the following day. Unlike *Evening Star*, *Morning Star* was to fade into oblivion and was scrapped some four months later, as were other stablemates at Carnforth during this Christmas and New Year holiday period. Just one Britannia, no. 70013 *Oliver Cromwell*, was to remain in service until the end of steam in August 1968 and is now preserved as part of the National Railway Museum's National Collection. Carnforth shed would never witness another sight such as this and would never be the same again. (Gordon Edgar)

68. The north end of Carnforth shed was photographed on 20th April 1968 showing the location of the turntable. (ColourRail.com)

69.   Standing on the first road of the running shed on 17th June 1972, from left to right, are Sentinel vertical boiler (works no. 8024 built in 1929) 0-4-0 *Gasbag*; Andrew Barclay (w/no. 1969 built 1929) 0-4-0ST *Jane Darbyshire*, now *J. N. Derbyshire*; both now reside at the Ribble Steam Railway, Preston. Next in line is Andrew Barclay (w/no. 2134 built 1942) 0-4-0ST *Toby*, originally named *W. T. T.* then *Toby* later *Coronation* and finally *W. T. T.* once more and it remains at Carnforth. Last in line is Hunslet 2-6-2T (w/no. 901 built in 1906) *Russell*, built to 1ft 11½ in gauge, now resident on the Welsh Highland Railway. (Gordon Edgar)

70. On 30th March 1976 locomotive Deutsche Reichsbahn (East Germany) 0-6-0T no. 80014, built by R. Wolf in 1927, is standing alongside the German 4-6-2 no. 012 104-6. Both locomotives were repatriated to Germany in around 2000 and are residents of the South German Railway Museum in Heilbronn, Baden-Württemberg. (Tom Heavyside)

71. On 24th April 1976 this shot records a busy day at Steamtown. Locomotives on display were MR class 4P 4-4-0 compound no. 1000, LNWR Precedent class 2-4-0 no. 790 *Hardwicke*, LNER class A3 4-6-2 no. 4472 *Flying Scotsman* and BR class 03 0-6-0 shunter no. D2381 that remains at Carnforth as a shunter for West Coast Railways. The Midland compound and the LNWR 790 had arrived from York on a rail tour that returned hauled by 4472. The signal box is 'Carnforth Station Junction' that is still in operation today. (Ron Herbert)

72. Bassett Lowke 15in gauge Atlantic 4-4-2 no. 18 is giving rides on 17th June 1979; the locomotive is now a resident of California. (Tom Heavyside)

→ 73. Lancashire and York-shire Railway class 27 0-6-0 no. 1300 is hauling coaches for train rides on 31st May 1982. (Tom Heavyside)

74. Ex-LMS Stanier 8F 2-8-0 no. 48151 takes centre stage in this shot taken on 3rd November 1990. To the left is is former SNCF Chapelon-built class 231K 4-6-2 no. 231K22 and, to the right, ex-Southern Railway Maunsell Lord Nelson class 7P 4-6-0 no. 850 *Lord Nelson*. (Tom Heavyside)

West Coast Railways

West Coast Railways (WCR) has been a licensed Train Operating Company since 1998, when it became the first privately-owned company to obtain a licence under rail privatisation and ran the Jacobite service from Fort William. Based at Carnforth, WCR currently operates several regular timetabled services, which, together with its other charter operations, amount to some 800 train operations a year. The company is now the UK market leader in operating steam and other charter services. The following seven photographs were all taken during organised visits to the WCR complex and illustrate some of the Railway's behind-the-scenes activities.

75. This view was taken on 17th June 2017 from the pedestrian access to Carnforth shed from the footbridge (since demolished) that deposited visitors right outside the shed foreman's office. In addition to the coaches there is a line of stored class 47s, nos 47851 *Traction Magazine*, 47787 *Windsor Castle*, an unidentified class member in yellow primer and BR class 57 no. 57004 that was rebuilt from a redundant class 47 by Brush Traction. (Gordon Edgar)

76. Jubilee class no. 45699 *Galatea* is in crimson lake in the wheel lathe shop on 18th May 2019. (Gordon Edgar)

77. Gresley Pacific no. 60009 *Union of South Africa* and Coronation class no. 46233 *Duchess of Sutherland* were photographed on shed on 18th May 2019. (Gordon Edgar)

78. Visiting a working steam shed nowadays is a rare treat, especially with such an opportunity on 4th September 2021 for capturing Royal Scot class no. 46115 *Scots Guardsman* outside with the coaling tower looming in the background. After receiving smoke deflectors, it starred in the 1936 film *Night Mail*. It was, in fact, the first member of the class to be equipped with the distinctive curved smoke deflectors. Standing alongside and completing the 1960s period reminder is 204hp class 03 shunter D2084 TOPS no. 03084. (Gordon Edgar)

79. Stanier Jubilee class 4-6-0 no. 45699, masquerading as no. 45627 *Sierra Leone,* moves across the turntable in preparation to take over the 'Cumbrian Mountain Express' charter from London Euston to Carlisle on Saturday 4th September 2021. On the right are WCR's class 57 no. 57315, class 37 no. 37676 *Loch Rannoch* and former Railway Operations Group class 47 no. 47812 in blue livery. (Gordon Edgar)

80. Class 47s nos 47832, 47245 and 47760 dominate class 57 no. 57313 and BR class 86 no. 86401 inside Carnforth Traction Maintenance Depot on 26th March 2022. No. 86401 was the only AC electric locomotive to legitimately carry Network SouthEast livery. (Gordon Edgar)

81. The locomotive in this picture, taken on 15th September 2022, is in fact Jubilee no. 45699 *Galatea* again. It also sported no. 45562 on the cab sides and no. 45627 on the smoke box door with matching *Sierra Leone* nameplates on occasion, although it did run with no. 45562 smoke box number and *Alberta* nameplates for a year or so. Alongside is ex-LMS Stanier Princess Royal class 4-6-2 *Princess Elizabeth* in LMS crimson lake bearing its original number 6201. (Gordon Edgar)

BURTON & HOLME

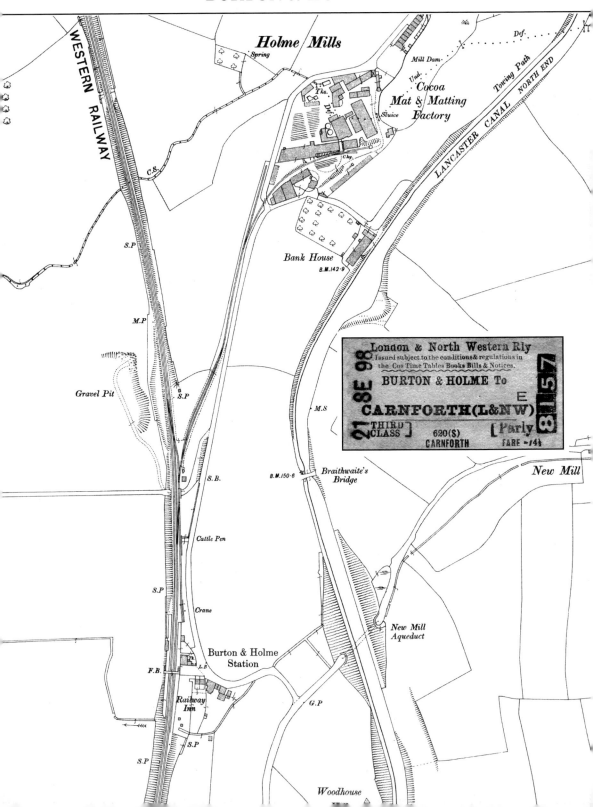

Holme Mills

Spring

Und.

Mill Dam

Cocoa
Mat & Matting
Factory

Sluice

WESTERN RAILWAY

C.S.

S.P

M.P

Gravel Pit

S.P

S.B.

Cattle Pen

S.P

Crane

F.B.

Burton & Holme
Station

Railway
Inn

S.P

S.P

Bank House
B.M.142·9

LANCASTER CANAL NORTH END

Towing Path

Def.

New Mill

B.M.150·6

Braithwaite's
Bridge

M.S

New Mill
Aqueduct

G.P

Woodhouse

XIV. Opened by the L&CR on 22nd September 1846, and located about a mile west of Burton-in-Kendal and a mile south of Holme, the station was somewhat remote. This 1914 map shows the small goods yard and, just to the north, a siding into the Holme Mills matting factory. The station building remains to this day as a private dwelling as does the The Old Station Inn, although it has been subject to a number of name changes over the years. The station closed to passengers on 25th March 1950 and to goods on 28th March 1966.

82. An undated view of the station looking north with all buildings bar a shelter on the up side. (Robert Humm collection)

83. It appears that all the station staff have turned out for this early but undated shot. Station seating is noticeable by its absence. (John Alsop collection)

MILNTHORPE

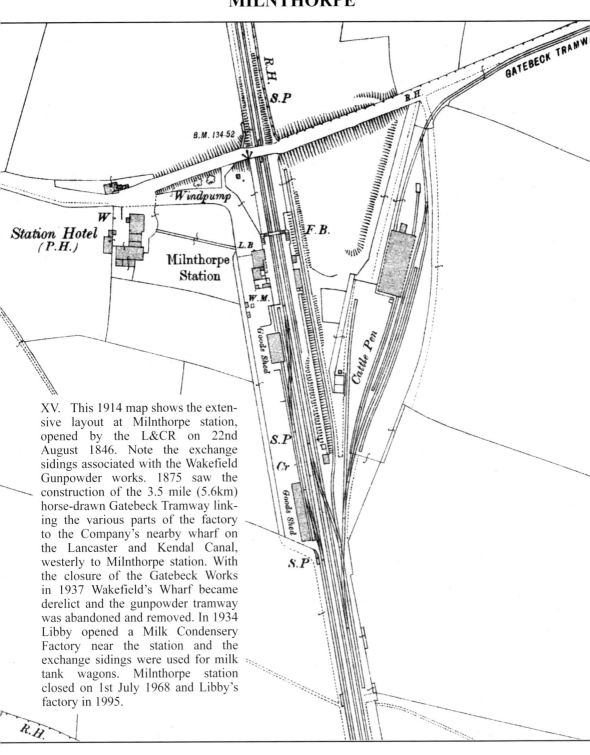

XV. This 1914 map shows the extensive layout at Milnthorpe station, opened by the L&CR on 22nd August 1846. Note the exchange sidings associated with the Wakefield Gunpowder works. 1875 saw the construction of the 3.5 mile (5.6km) horse-drawn Gatebeck Tramway linking the various parts of the factory to the Company's nearby wharf on the Lancaster and Kendal Canal, westerly to Milnthorpe station. With the closure of the Gatebeck Works in 1937 Wakefield's Wharf became derelict and the gunpowder tramway was abandoned and removed. In 1934 Libby opened a Milk Condensery Factory near the station and the exchange sidings were used for milk tank wagons. Milnthorpe station closed on 1st July 1968 and Libby's factory in 1995.

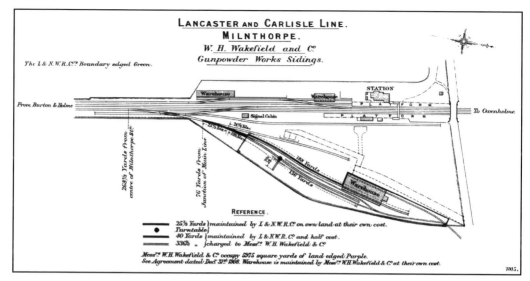

XVI. Track diagram of the Gunpowder Works Sidings, courtesy of Cumbrian Railway Association.

← *Built by Hurst Nelson & Co Ltd of Motherwell, this van was owned by W.H. Wakefield & Co Ltd and had a load capacity of 7 tons. (Cumbrian Railway Association)*

84. The main station building in this picture, although undated, is likely to be around the date of closure in 1968. (ColourRail.com)

85. Station staff pose for this undated picture of the station looking north. (John Alsop collection)

86. Britannia class no. 70039 *Sir Christopher Wren*, by then bereft of its nameplates, heads north with a mixed freight service some time in the 1960s. In the sidings to the left are milk tanks associated with the Libby's factory. (ColourRail.com)

87. View looking north with an unidentified Brush Type 4 passing on an up service on 22nd October 1966. Note the Wickham Permanent Way trolley in the siding. (Peter Fidczuk collection)

Hincaster Junction

88. This view of the junction looks north from the train en route from the Arnside line, converging with the WCML to the right. This was the regular route of the Windermere portion of summer Saturday services from Leeds that had divided at Arnside as recorded on 28th July 1962. Regular passenger services were suspended during WWII and were never reinstated. The locomotive is ex-LMS Stanier class 4MT 2-6-4T no. 42483. (Roger Joanes)

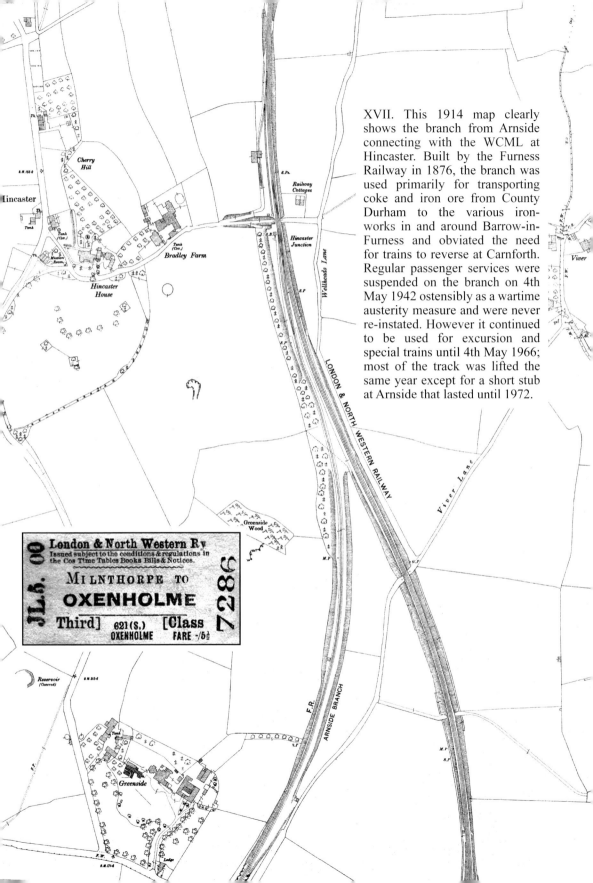

XVII. This 1914 map clearly shows the branch from Arnside connecting with the WCML at Hincaster. Built by the Furness Railway in 1876, the branch was used primarily for transporting coke and iron ore from County Durham to the various ironworks in and around Barrow-in-Furness and obviated the need for trains to reverse at Carnforth. Regular passenger services were suspended on the branch on 4th May 1942 ostensibly as a wartime austerity measure and were never re-instated. However it continued to be used for excursion and special trains until 4th May 1966; most of the track was lifted the same year except for a short stub at Arnside that lasted until 1972.

London & North Western Rᵧ
Issued subject to the conditions & regulations in the Cos Time Tables Books Bills & Notices.

MILNTHORPE TO
OXENHOLME

Third]   621(S.)   [Class
OXENHOLME   FARE -/5½

JLS. 00

7286

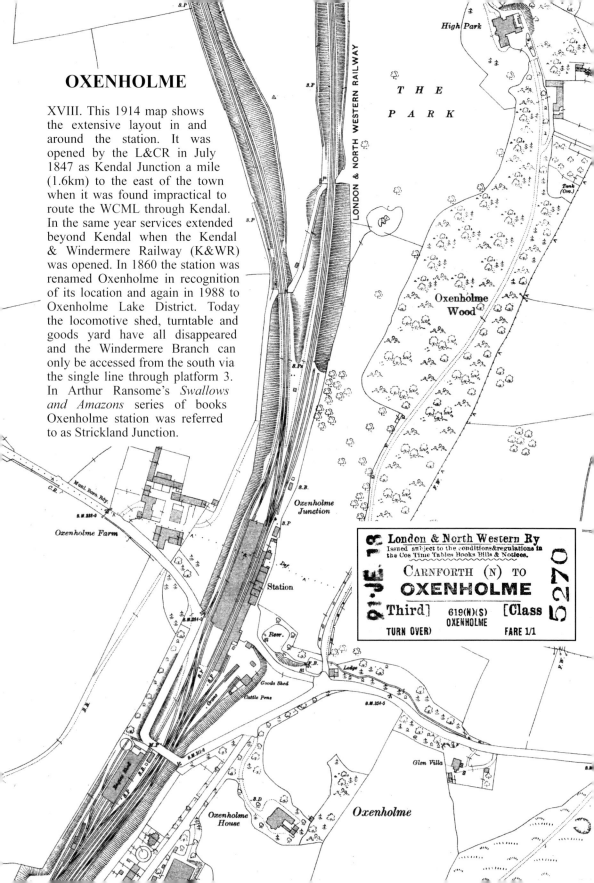

OXENHOLME

XVIII. This 1914 map shows the extensive layout in and around the station. It was opened by the L&CR in July 1847 as Kendal Junction a mile (1.6km) to the east of the town when it was found impractical to route the WCML through Kendal. In the same year services extended beyond Kendal when the Kendal & Windermere Railway (K&WR) was opened. In 1860 the station was renamed Oxenholme in recognition of its location and again in 1988 to Oxenholme Lake District. Today the locomotive shed, turntable and goods yard have all disappeared and the Windermere Branch can only be accessed from the south via the single line through platform 3. In Arthur Ransome's *Swallows and Amazons* series of books Oxenholme station was referred to as Strickland Junction.

LONDON & NORTH WESTERN RAILWAY

THE PARK

High Park

Tank (Cov.)

Oxenholme Wood

Oxenholme Junction

Oxenholme Farm

Station

Goods Shed

Cattle Pens

Glen Villa

Oxenholme House

Oxenholme

London & North Western Ry
Issued subject to the conditions & regulations in the Cos Time Tables Books Bills & Notices.
CARNFORTH (N) TO
OXENHOLME
Third] 619(N)(S) [Class
OXENHOLME
TURN OVER) FARE 1/1

21 JE 13

5270

89. Although shorn of its sidings, and with the branch to Windermere now singled and the main line electrified, very little of the landscape has changed since the 1914 map on the previous page was published. CAF class 397 Civity EMU no. 397001 departs with the Lancaster - Glasgow service as CAF class 195, also of the Civity family, DMU no. 195102 sets off with the 12.39 Oxenholme - Windermere service on 24th September 2022. The former engine shed would have been further south of the car park at the bottom left of the image. The circles marked on the grass slope to the left of the station belong to Kendal Golf Driving Range. (Tom McAtee)

90. An undated photograph of Oxenholme shed looking north and which was opened in 1880 and closed to steam on 18th June 1962. (John Alsop collection)

91. An unidentified Webb LNWR 2-2-2-2 locomotive is waiting to depart from platform 1 in this undated photograph. Under the Whyte notation for the classification of steam locomotives, the wheel arrangement was of two leading wheels, four powered but uncoupled driving wheels and two trailing wheels. Webb's two classes of 2-2-2-2s were built in the last decade of the 19th century but were so unreliable they were scrapped in the first decade of the 20th. (John Alsop collection)

92. The driver and fireman look out of the cab of the rebuilt Patriot class no. 45545 *Planet* waiting for the road to clear to allow them to continue their journey with the 8.10am service from Windermere to Manchester Exchange. The train has stopped at platform 3 awaiting the passage of a northbound stopping train to Carlisle calling at platform 2, from which this photograph was taken on 23rd April 1960. The Patriot was named and rebuilt in 1948 with a large taper boiler, new cylinders and double chimney. (Noel Machell)

OXENHOLME, KENDAL, BURNESIDE, and WINDERMERE.—L. M. & S.

Down. — Week Days. / Suns.

Miles	Station		
	Oxenholme .....dep.		
2	Kendal		
4	Burneside		
6¼	Staveley		
10¼	Windermere ‖..arr.		

Up. — Week Days. / Suns.

Miles	Station		
	Windermere ...dep.		
3¾	Staveley		
6¼	Burneside		
8¼	Kendal		
10¼	Oxenholme .....arr.		

A Except Wednesdays and Thursdays.   B Except Mondays and Saturdays.   D Mondays and Saturdays.   E Except Saturdays.
H Except Thursdays and Saturdays.   K Thursdays and Saturdays.   S or s Saturdays only.
‖ Station for Bowness (1¼ miles) and Ambleside (4¼ miles).

July 1924

93. Ex-LMS Fowler Patriot class no. 45516 *The Bedfordshire and Hertfordshire Regiment* is passing through platform 2 with a down freight on 30th April 1960. Note the Windermere service waiting in platform 3. (ColourRail.com)

94. Split headcode class 40 no. D333 (TOPS no. 40133) signalled to depart for the south on 22nd December 1962. The crane, seen to the right of the picture, was of 5 ton capacity. (ColourRail.com)

95. Britannia class no 70016 *Ariel* runs briskly into platform 2 with the 11.55 London Euston - Carlisle and Windermere Saturdays only service on 1st July 1967. The train was split at Oxenholme with the rear portion taken to Windermere by Black 5 no. 45445. The signal box, Oxenholme No. 2, closed on 12th May 1973; it had approximately 60 levers. (Robin McGregor)

96. An unidentified BR class 108 DMU stands in platform 3 on 7th October 1983 for a Windermere service. The overall roof remains to this day but was not always appreciated. It seems that some passengers ignored the 'do not flush in the station' notice, which led to unpleasant odours under the roof at times. (ColourRail.com/S.R. Lee)

97. Pacer no. 143601 forms the 13.25 Windermere - Oxenholme service on 1st December 1990. It is slowing for the stop as it nears the top of the climb up the gradient from Kendal to the junction with the WCML. Note the old style BR maroon sign to the left of the picture indicating the line leading to Kendal and Windermere. At the time the DMU was based at Heaton depot, Newcastle-on-Tyne. (Noel Machell)

98. Built at Brighton and originally allocated to Tunbridge Wells West depot, it must have been a culture shock to BR Fairburn class 4 2-6-4T no. 42098 having to spend its latter days employed banking freight trains from Oxenholme to Grayrigg summit, high up in the Westmorland fell country. Here we see 42098 buffered up to the rear of a northbound freight awaiting the 'right away' before tackling this exacting turn of duty in the early evening of 9th September 1961. Unfortunately, the identity of the train engine, which appears to have built up a good fire, is unknown. (Noel Machell)

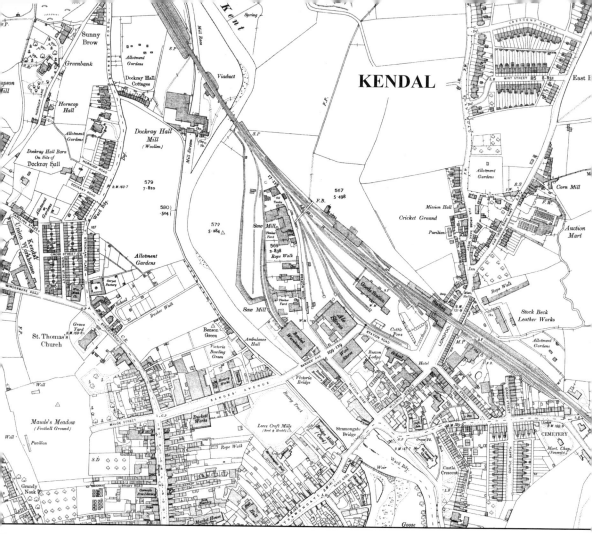

KENDAL

XIX. This 1914 map shows the extensive layout at Kendal, which is now reduced to a single platform with all trace of the sidings gone. The station was opened on 28th September 1846 and was the temporary terminus of the L&CR. With the formation of the K&WR Kendal became a through station on 20th April 1847. In May 1973 the line was singled and the Oxenholme platform and other buildings demolished; the station building remains but is home to a commercial enterprise and the site of the former down platform is a car park.

← 99. The 14.40 Windermere - Oxenholme service on 8th February 1992, operated by Pacer no. 143615, approaches Kendal station with the photograph showing the front of this attractive station building that is now in private commercial use. (Noel Machell)

100. Black 5 no. 45431 with a train bound for Windermere on 1st August 1962. (Roger Joanes)

101. The final months of the 'pick-up' freight in Westmorland. Black 5 no. 45054 shunts the Windermere branch freight at Kendal on 23rd December 1967. The Black 5 was withdrawn from service just two months later. One can only speculate on the contents of the barrels.
(Eric F. Bentley/Gordon Edgar collection)

102. In this view of Kendal station, class 156 no. 156427, based at Newton Heath, stands waiting to travel on to Windermere with the 15.36 departure from Oxenholme on Saturday 11th May 1996. The old station building, constructed of slate with limestone dressings, blends in well with the surrounding urban backdrop. The former up line was removed and is now a car park. The difference in level between the Lakes line at this point and the WCML can be judged as the latter is visible in the background running between the two small white buildings below the skyline of the far hillside. (Noel Machell)

103. On 22nd June 2018 West Coast Railway's class 47 no. 47245, sporting 'The Lakelander' nameboard, pulls out of Kendal bound for Windermere. WCR stepped in to provide rail services between Oxenholme and Windermere after the operator Northern cancelled all of its trains following the timetabling fiasco. Using vintage diesel locomotives and coaching stock along the 10 mile route, WCR ran trains six times a day, from 09.25 to 19.00. It is understood that the Department for Transport met the £5,500 daily cost of running the service. (Gary Lewis)

104. The Windermere branch crosses the River Kent just north of Kendal station and, here, the 16.04 Oxenholme - Windermere service is pictured crossing the viaduct on 14th July 1984; the train was formed of two BR class 108 twin car DMUs. While the photograph depicts the Kent as a slow flowing river, during wet and stormy weather it can resemble a raging torrent capable, at times, of flooding parts of Kendal and most notably in December 2015 as a consequence of Storm Desmond. (Noel Machell)

BURNESIDE

105. Perhaps the most distinctive feature of the station is the staggered platform arrangement as seen in this circa 1910 shot looking in the Windermere direction. (LOSA)

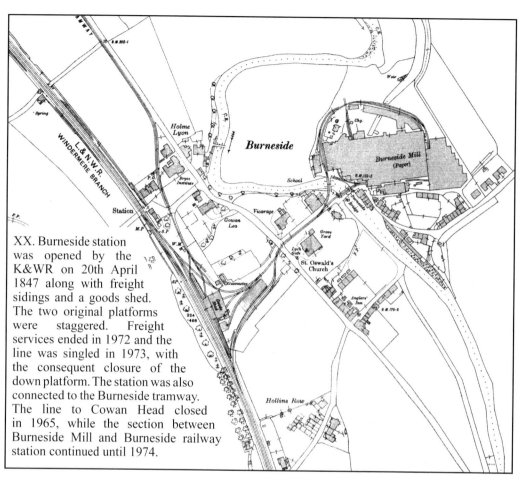

XX. Burneside station was opened by the K&WR on 20th April 1847 along with freight sidings and a goods shed. The two original platforms were staggered. Freight services ended in 1972 and the line was singled in 1973, with the consequent closure of the down platform. The station was also connected to the Burneside tramway. The line to Cowan Head closed in 1965, while the section between Burneside Mill and Burneside railway station continued until 1974.

106. Ex-LMS Stanier class 4MT 2-6-4T no. 42613 arrives with a train bound for Oxenholme on 28th July 1962. The staggered platform arrangement is well illustrated in this shot. The small building on the right housed the General Waiting Room and Ladies toilets. (Roger Joanes)

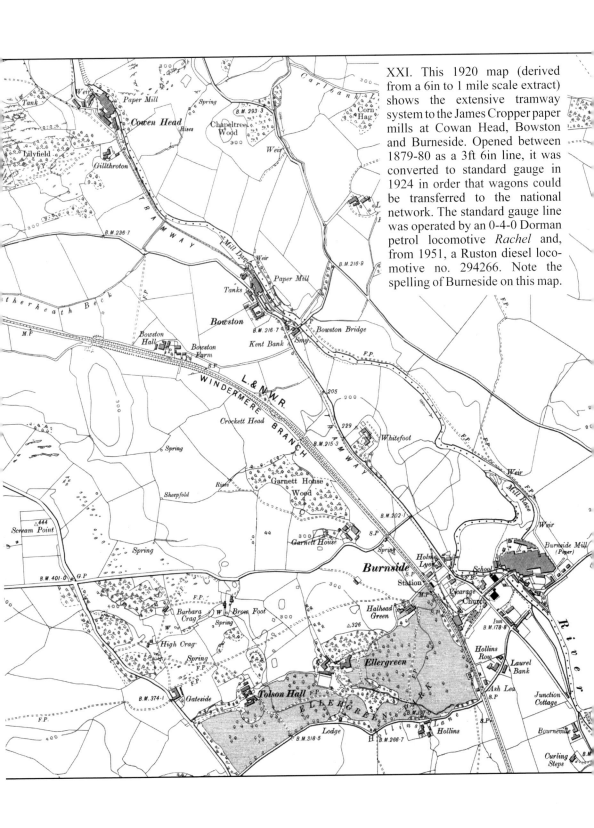

XXI. This 1920 map (derived from a 6in to 1 mile scale extract) shows the extensive tramway system to the James Cropper paper mills at Cowan Head, Bowston and Burneside. Opened between 1879-80 as a 3ft 6in line, it was converted to standard gauge in 1924 in order that wagons could be transferred to the national network. The standard gauge line was operated by an 0-4-0 Dorman petrol locomotive *Rachel* and, from 1951, a Ruston diesel locomotive no. 294266. Note the spelling of Burneside on this map.

107. On this occasion, Pacer no. 143625 is approaching the station on 29th September 1990 with the 14.40 Windermere - Oxenholme service. Comparing this shot with the previous photograph there is now but a simple waiting shelter and the line has been singled but the telegraph poles remain in situ. (Noel Machell)

Burneside Paper Mills Tramway

108. Cropper-owned Dorman Petrol 0-4-0 *Rachel* with wagons, near Burneside, on the tramway from Cowan Head circa 1950. *Rachel* has survived and is preserved at the Lakeside and Haverthwaite Railway at the southern tip of Lake Windermere, Cumbria. (Cumbrian Railway Association)

109. In 1951 the aforementioned petrol locomotive was replaced by a Ruston 48 diesel 0-4-0 no. 294266, seen here by the churchyard between Burneside Mill and the BR station in around 1960. When the tramway closed, the Ruston locomotive was moved to Carnforth where it was named *Flying Flea*. It later moved south to Sir William McAlpine's Fawley Hill Railway, where it was renamed *Sir William*. After a spell at Laurie's Mechanical Marvels, Stowmarket, it was acquired by the Mid-Suffolk Light Railway and again renamed as *Sir William McAlpine* where it is involved with permanent way duties. (Cumbrian Railway Association)

Northwest of Burneside

110. A thin dusting of snow covers the tops of the fells above Staveley as a class 108 twin car DMU hurries towards Burneside with the 13.36 Windermere - Oxenholme working on the rather cold afternoon of 16th March 1985. (Noel Machell)

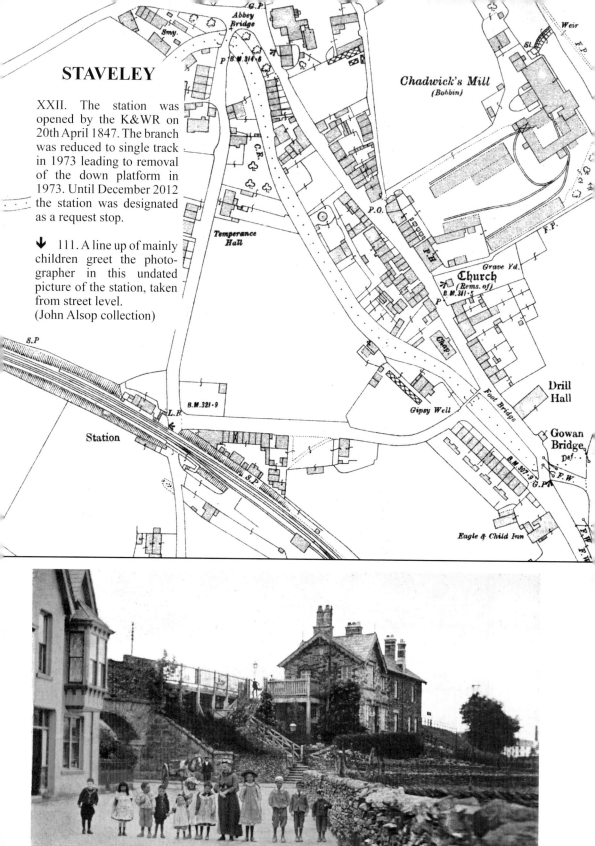

STAVELEY

XXII. The station was opened by the K&WR on 20th April 1847. The branch was reduced to single track in 1973 leading to removal of the down platform in 1973. Until December 2012 the station was designated as a request stop.

↓ 111. A line up of mainly children greet the photographer in this undated picture of the station, taken from street level. (John Alsop collection)

Abbey Bridge

Smy.

G.P.

Chadwick's Mill
(Bobbin)

Weir

F.P.

C.R.

P.O.

Temperance Hall

P.H

Grave Yd.

Church
(Rems. of)

B.M.311·5

F.P.

Chap.

Station

B.M.321·9

L.B

S.P

Gipsy Well

Foot Bridge

Drill Hall

Gowan Bridge

Def.

F.W.

B.M.307·9

G.P

Eagle & Child Inn

112. A deserted station looking towards Oxenholme in 1972, not long before the line was singled. (LOSA)

113. Seen from Reston Scar, overlooking Staveley, a Siemens built First TransPennine Express Desiro class 185 DMU passes Staveley Crossing on 25th March 2018 with an Oxenholme - Windermere service. (Duncan Robert)

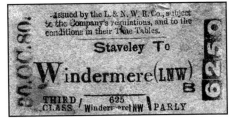

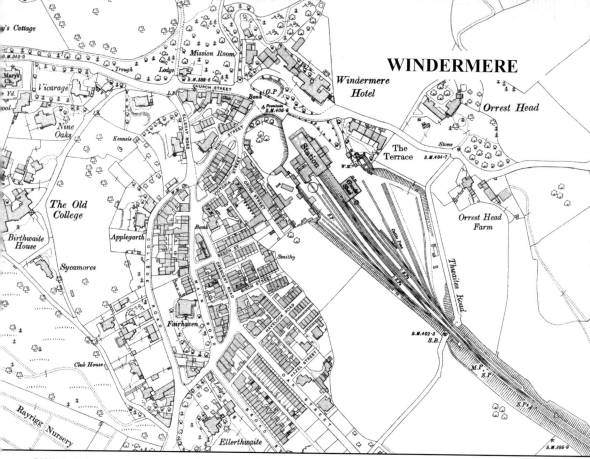

XXIII. Windermere did not exist as a village until the advent of the railways. Opened by the K&WR on 20th April 1847, this was the terminus of the branch from Oxenholme. The station had three platforms, an overall roof, a goods yard, a shed and a turntable. Today the station is just a single line and platform. The former station buildings and surrounding land are now occupied by a supermarket and a national retailer.

114. This impressive shot of the station circa 1910 is now a supermarket entrance with access to the now single platform further down the left-hand side of the building. (LOSA)

↑ *Bradshaw advertisement, August 1898.*

115. This shot was taken inside the station with its overall roof and empty stock in the centre road looking along platform 2 away from the buffers. While the photo is undated, interesting front pages on the newsstand report on General Botha's farewell, which pins it down to July 1904. (LOSA)

116. Ex-LNWR Precedent class 2-4-0 no. 2187 was built in 1896 and in 1924 was renumbered 5069. It was repainted in LMS maroon livery and very appropriately named *Penrith Beacon*. In this undated photo it is standing in platform 2. The locomotive was withdrawn in 1932. (LOSA)

117. Ex-LMS Crab 2-6-0 no. 42838 is with a service about to depart for Preston on 29th July 1962. (Roger Joanes)

118.   Black 5 no. 45077 is on the turntable in July 1963 just south of the main station buildings. (ColourRail.com)

119. Built by English Electric, BR class 50 Co-Co no. 430 (TOPS no. 50030) has arrived with the daily 1P18 09.05 London Euston - Windermere service in April 1969 having taken over at Crewe. It was named *Repulse* on 10th April 1978 and is now owned by the RenownRepulse Restoration Group based at Peak Rail, Derbyshire. (ColourRail.com/G. Parry collection)

120. With the Windermere Hotel dominating the background, two Pacer class 142 units depart from Windermere station with the 15.05 train to Oxenholme on 28th May 1987. To the right through the trees one can just see the former cottages built in 1849 for executives of the K&WR, the design of which has been loosely attributed to Pugin whose other works include the Palace of Westminster. The Provincial sector two-tone blue and white livery really suited these units giving them a most attractive external appearance, belying their mediocre passenger experience. (Noel Machell)